MARCO  POLO

Travel with
Insider Tips

MADEIRA

PORTO SANTO

Atlantic
Ocean

Azores (Port.)

PORTUGAL

Madeira
(Portugal)

MOROCCO

Canary Isles
(Spain)

Western
Sahara

D0675545

SYMBOLS

INSIDER TIP Insider Tip

★ Highlight

●●●● Best of ...

☼ Scenic view

☺ Responsible travel: for ecological or fair trade aspects

(*) Telephone numbers
that are not toll-free

**PRICE CATEGORIES
HOTELS**

Expensive over 100 euros

Moderate 60–100 euros

Budget under 60 euros

Prices per night for two
persons in double room with
breakfast in season

**PRICE CATEGORIES
RESTAURANTS**

Expensive over 18 euros

Moderate 12–18 euros

Budget under 12 euros

Prices for a meal with
starter, main course and
dessert, without drinks

On the cover: Casa das Mudas p. 52 | Lava pools in Porto Moniz p. 62

CONTENTS

The North → p. 60

The East → p. 70

Porto Santo → p. 80

Road atlas → p. 118

MAPS IN THE GUIDEBOOK
(120 A1) Page numbers and coordinates refer to the road atlas
(0) Site/address located off the map. Coordinates are also given for places that are not marked on the road atlas
A street map of Funchal and a map of the bus routes on Madeira can be found inside the back cover

**INSIDE BACK COVER:
PULL-OUT MAP →**

PULL-OUT MAP 🗺
(🗺 A–B 2–3) refers to the pull-out map

The best MARCO POLO Insider Tips

Our top 15 Insider Tips

INSIDER TIP **Music in Funchal**

FNAC Funchal is a place for fans of books or music to browse. The store has a wide range of Portuguese, Brazilian and international music, as well as a variety of music and cultural events on the stage of the café → **p. 41**

INSIDER TIP **Yearn no more**

Chega de Saudade ('enough yearning') in Funchal is the rendezvous for artists and art-lovers, who can enjoy a delicious dinner and a glass of good wine while listening to live jazz, and then make a bid for the antique furnishings → **p. 42**

INSIDER TIP **Nuns' retreat**

The cemetery of Curral das Freiras provides not only an interesting insight into Madeiran burial traditions, but also a spectacular view of the mountains around the 'valley of the nuns' → **p. 46**

INSIDER TIP **A drink in the mill**

For the local cocktail made from lemon juice, sugar-cane spirit and honey, Madeirans come from far and wide to the Bar Moinho (mill), where the *poncha* tastes terrific → **p. 57**

INSIDER TIP **Raid the garden**

In the organic orchard and vegetable garden of the Quinta do Cabouco, hotel guests are allowed to help themselves for free, and their hosts are happy to explain what the exotic fruits are → **p. 58**

INSIDER TIP **Forest path for the blind**

From the Pico das Pedras a one-hour trail that was made for the blind leads to the forest lodge of Queimadas – along a levada and through lush laurel forest (photo left) → **p. 66**

INSIDER TIP **Unspoiled view**

A wide-ranging panorama from the Ponta Vigia lookout point on the north coast of Madeira → **p. 66**

INSIDER TIP **Snorkellers' paradise**
When the beach of Porto Santo is too crowded, snorkellers go down to the remote rocky bay of Zimbralinho, where they find turquoise water and peace → p. 85

INSIDER TIP **Horsepower on the beach**
Discover the hills and beaches of Porto Santo on horseback: Centro Hipico also organises riding tours for children and beginners → p. 85

INSIDER TIP **A fairytale park**
An abundant mixture of local and exotic fauna, works of art from five centuries, a collection of minerals and an Asian garden with koi carp delight visitors to the tropical palace garden in Monte (photo right) → p. 48

INSIDER TIP **To honour Saint Peter**
The people of Porto Santo hold an impressive celebration for the patron saint of fishermen → p. 89

INSIDER TIP **Tea and golf**
In the Quinta Serra Golf, once the tea parlour of Santo da Serra, you can still take your afternoon tea in style – whether you want to play golf or not → p. 78

INSIDER TIP **Madeira from the air**
A bird's eye view of the island is unforgettable. Take off from the Paragliding Center in Arco da Calheta and fly over Madeira → p. 53

INSIDER TIP **Sail to a desert island**
On a day trip to the uninhabited nature reserve of the Ilhas Desertas you can spot sea birds, dolphins, whales and sometimes even monk seals → p. 98

INSIDER TIP **The old market hall**
Dine well in historic surroundings: the food is excellent at Café Mercado Velho by the old fountain in Machico → p. 75

BEST OF ...

FOR FREE

● *A garden to die for*
The *Quinta Splendida* hotel in Caniço has a wonderful garden, in which many plants are labelled. Non-residents too can enjoy its beauty and the ocean view (photo) → p. 46

● *Live like Asterix*
The village of Santana is reminiscent of a Gallic settlement: although the thatched houses are no longer inhabited today, visitors can take a look around and find some great photo opportunities → p. 63

● *Cape Turnaround*
Cabo Girão made such an impression on the first settlers that they initially turned back: this is where Madeira drops a sheer 580 m (630 yd) into the sea. Don't miss this spectacular view – a white-knuckle experience, free of charge → p. 44

● *Churches with gold and tiles*
Though Madeira's churches and chapels are often plain and unassuming from the outside, within they are resplendent in the glory of *talha dourada* (gilded carvings) and historic tile pictures. The village church of São Jorge is an especially fine example → p. 66

● *Admire some embroidery*
The *Casa do Turista* is almost a museum of arts and crafts: selected Madeira embroidery work is on display alongside other craft products in attractively decorated rooms in Funchal. Visitors are extremely welcome just to come and admire these precious artefacts. There is Madeira wine in the next room → p. 40

● *Fresh trout by a sparkling stream*
The stream called *Ribeiro Frio* supplies water to prettily located trout ponds. Here you can see how the fish develop – from baby trout that are just 5 mm long to huge, rather splendid specimens → p. 73

◯◯◯◯● Dots in guidebook refer to 'Best of ...' tips

● *Colourful and varied delicacies*

Flowers in glowing colours, exotic fruit, delicious vegetables and fresh fish – these are the treasures of Madeira. Tastefully arranged so that you can try them and take photos, they are on display in the *Mercado dos Lavradores* in Funchal. Friday is the liveliest market day (photo) → p. 36

● *Island of eternal spring*

In Funchal's *Jardim Botânico* you can enjoy a blaze of colour at any time of year. And when you have seen all the plants, flowers and cacti, take the cable car to Monte and admire what's growing there → p. 46

● *Sleds without snow*

Take a basket sled on runners, propelled by the muscles of strong men, along the road from Monte down towards Funchal – a tradition that's over 100 years old → p. 48

● *Along the levadas*

Walk by the side of ancient irrigation channels through woods of eucalyptus and laurel, past dizzying gorges or along broad forest tracks: there are many tours for walkers on the levadas of Madeira, for example on the *Levada do Furado* → p. 73

● *Favourite local dishes: espada and espetada*

Madeira's national dishes are truly delicious – try black scabbard fish with banana in the *Borda d'Água* in Ribeira Brava. *Espetada,* juicy chunks of beef on a laurel-wood skewer, is served in traditional style at the *Miradouro da Portela* on the Portela Pass → p. 58, 78

● *Santa Maria de Colombo*

Christopher Columbus lived on Madeira for a few years and planned his voyages here. On a replica of his ship, built true to the original, you can feel like the discoverer of America → p. 100

● *Swimming pool in the volcanic rock*

The natural lava pools in Porto Moniz are refreshing and unique. And don't worry – there are changing rooms! → p. 62

ONLY IN

BEST OF ...

RAIN

● *A journey back in time*
The Madeira Story Centre in Funchal is not only for children: its presentation of the island history is entertaining and interactive → p. 36

● *Inside the volcano*
In São Vicente you can take a guided tour through a fascinating system of lava tunnels. The visitor centre provides background information and all sorts of surprises → p. 67

● *See the fish without getting wet*
What used to be a fort in Porto Moniz is now home to an aquarium. Almost the whole marine life of Madeira swims about before your eyes in a variety of pools and tanks (photo) → p. 61

● *Whales and the history of whaling*
Until the 1980s Caniçal lived entirely from the whaling industry – and then the cruel whale fishery was banned. Today you can find out about the exciting history of whaling in a modern museum devoted to the subject → p. 76

● *Art and culture in Calheta*
The *Casa das Mudas* art centre has attracted much attention for its intriguing architecture. On top of that there are changing exhibitions, an innovative cultural programme and an excellent café-restaurant → p. 52

● *Under the surface*
Off the coast of Madeira between *Caniço de Baixo* and *Garajau* lies an underwater paradise where the marine fauna is protected. Several diving bases along the south coast offer try-dive courses and guided underwater expeditions → p. 97

RELAX AND CHILL OUT
Take it easy and spoil yourself

● *Pure relaxation in the Choupana Spa*
The spa at Choupana Hill Resort is regarded as the best in all Portugal. If you really want to be spoiled – and gaze on a spectacular view of Funchal at the same time – book one of the wellness packages → **p. 42**

● *The sound of mandolins*
During the season Madeira's mandolin orchestra gives a concert every Friday evening in the English Church in Funchal, and sometimes in the municipal theatre. The sound has enchanted many a visitor over the years → **p. 42**

● *It's tea time!*
Follow the example of Winston Churchill, George Bernard Shaw and Empress Elisabeth of Austria by enjoying the legendary afternoon tea on the terrace of *Reid´s* in Funchal – the scones and cakes are wonderful, and the view is magnificent (photo) → **p. 43**

● *A banquet fit for a noble knight*
For fine dining in the stylish ambience of a historic building, try the *São Tiago Fort* in Funchal, where diners enjoy a view out to sea. Sit back and savour the regional, national and international cuisine → **p. 40**

● *Chill out at the end of the cable car*
A small lift goes down the steep cliff to the alluvial plain called *Fajã dos Padres*. And if a meal of fish in the little restaurant or a swim all alone in the sea doesn't make the place feel secluded enough, then stay overnight and imagine you are Robinson Crusoe → **p. 44**

● *Health and beauty in the sand*
On Madeira's little sister, the island of Porto Santo, there are spas everywhere you look. The beach of *Campo de Baixo* with its fine-grained sand is just right for thalassotherapy. Get one of the experts to bury you in the sand → **p. 84**

INTRODUCTION

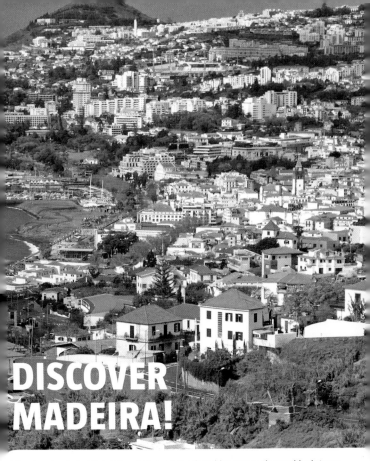

DISCOVER MADEIRA!

The plane banks boldly to take a left above the deep-blue waves, then suddenly turns to the right – and before you know it the wheels are touching the runway. *Bem vindo* – welcome to Madeira, the green pearl of the Atlantic! Madeira is breathtaking – and that even applies to landing at the airport, which is no longer a dangerous manoeuvre thanks to the extension and widening of the runway. Sometimes the Ponta de São Lourenço, the barren eastern tip of the island, appears unexpectedly out of the thick clouds to give a memorable first impression of this mountainous volcanic island, which covers an area of almost 800 sq km (310 sq mi).

It's true: Madeira's eternal spring is not a legend. But mild doesn't necessarily mean sunny, and there is a good reason why the vegetation is so lush and green. Not only that, but the island, which is only 22 km (14 mi) wide and 57 km (35 mi) long and lies at the same latitude as Casablanca some 900 km (560 mi) from its mother country Portugal, is marked by considerable variation in altitude. At Pico Ruivo (1862 m, 2040 yds), the highest of Madeira's weather-beaten lava peaks, the temperature

Photo: View of Funchal

Fruit and flowers in abundance: the island's riches are on show at the Mercado dos Lavradores

is always much lower than it is down by the coast. A cold wind often blows in the uplands and the exposed peninsulas – a fact emphasised by the numerous wind generators that now produce energy there. The moist trade winds often bring rain to the northern side of the island's mountains while at the same moment the weather is beautiful on the south side or at lower altitudes.

> **Madeira's laurisilva forest is a World Heritage site**

As long ago as the 15th century the first settlers took advantage of these geographical conditions by hewing narrow watercourses, *levadas,* into the rock in order to channel precious water from the rainy mountains to their sugar-cane fields. The *levada* system *func-*

1351
Madeira makes its first appearance on a navigation chart under the Italian name of *Isola di Legno* (island of wood)

1419–20
The seafarers João Gonçalves Zarco, Tristão Vaz Teixeira and Bartolomeu Perestrelo take possession of Porto Santo and Madeira for Portugal

about 1440
Prince Henry the Navigator orders the first Malvasia (Malmsey) grape vines to be taken from Crete to Madeira

from 1456
Exports of sugar bring art, wealth, merchants and slaves to Madeira

tions to this day. Most of today's channels were made in the second half of the 20th century, usually in association with small hydroelectric plants. The paths used for maintaining the levadas have become a popular and extensive network of walking trails. Along with the *veredas,* old cobbled paths, they lead from the coast, which falls steeply into the ocean and is rocky and rugged in many places, to the green heart of the island with its wild gorges and geological formations that are millions of years old. There is a superb new panoramic view round almost every bend – especially in the northwest, where much of the original laurisilva forest, which UNESCO declared a World Heritage site, has been preserved.

Whether you like walking or playing golf, hang-gliding, windsurfing or diving, climbing, canyoning or mountainbiking – in terms of sports, Madeira has it all. There are now even beaches of golden sand on this volcanic island – created, admittedly, using sand

Lava pools and sandy beaches

from Morocco. Until a few years ago the islanders and sun-seeking tourists had to cross to the neighbouring island of Porto Santo if they wanted to build a sandcastle. Today those who feel like a dip in the Atlantic can decide whether they would rather spend a day on the yellow sandy beach in Calheta or Machico, or enjoy the more traditional beaches of pebbles or black sand, for example in Funchal, or even enter the water by means of ladders in natural lava pools. If you are looking for miles of sand, then Porto Santo is still the best place to go. It's just a short hop by air or a two-hour crossing by ferry to Madeira's sister island. Along with the Ilhas Desertas some 30 km (19 mi) to the southeast and the Ilhas Selvagens, which are also uninhabited and lie approximately 250 km (155 mi) away, these two dissimilar islands make up the Madeiran archipelago.

Madeira's natural beauty has many sides. There are almost 800 different species of native plants and more than 500 imported species on the island, two thirds of which has been designated a natural park since the 1980s. In its subtropical climate grapes for wine, bananas and a great many other exotic fruits grow extremely well on its terraced fields. In the mountains aromatic wild herbs are to be found, and flowers of all shapes and colours line the serpentine roads. In the early 19th century rich English families who had settled on Madeira vied with each other to cultivate the loveliest and most unusual *jardins.* The island's famous gardens and parks were thus created

1497
Funchal becomes the sole island capital; previously Madeira was ruled from Funchal and Machico

1580–1640
Portugal comes under Spanish rule after an interruption in the line of succession to the Portuguese throne

1703
Portugal and England sign a treaty on commercial relations. In the following period English merchants take control of the Madeiran wine trade

1801–07
British soldiers are based on Madeira during the Napoleonic Wars

Kings, emperors and artists came to the island

around the family estates – and many of them are open to visitors today.

It was not long before the British also dominated the Madeiran economy. Under their influence both the wine trade and tourism prospered. The latter is now – directly or indirectly – the source of earnings for most of Madeira's 260,000 inhabitants. Agriculture is becoming less and less important, as many young Madeirans are reluctant to take on arduous work in the terraced fields for poor returns. They prefer to move to the towns, where they work in the tourist business or other jobs in the service sector. For the older generation, too, rural life is hard because the *poios,* the narrow terraced strips, can usually only be cultivated using hoes and sickles. In the past the farmers personally travelled to the capital by donkey or boat to sell what they harvested, but now purchasers from the cooperatives do the rounds of the villages in their trucks. As there were hardly any roads on the island for a long time, tourism was mostly restricted to the capital, Funchal. The first tourist boom happened in the late 19th and early 20th century, when emperors, kings and artists all wanted to spend part of the year on the 'island of flowers'. Many of them were following their doctor's advice: Madeira's constant, mild, wet climate was seen as excellent medicine for respiratory complaints, heart disease and 'nervous disorders'. Empress Elisabeth of Austria was probably the most prominent among those who came to the island in search of recuperation.

The people of Madeira are helpful and willing

In the 21st century the theme of physical well-being again came to the fore in marketing the island's benefits. Health, fitness and relaxation are the new buzzwords, and new hotel complexes with

spa facilities are springing up everywhere – not only in Funchal. However, so far the island's only large town has also remained the centre of the tourism industry, which is why Funchal is expanding on all sides of its charming historic centre with an ever-growing belt of modern architecture. New areas of housing are creeping up the slopes into the mountains, because young people are crowding into the city despite the high rents. This marked spread of settlement in the south of Madeira caused problems in February 2010, when heavy storms turned small mountain streams into swollen, raging torrents. Although the people of Madeira immediately showed their solidarity and

1947 Scheduled air connections between Portugal and Madeira using flying boats

1960 Opening of the airport on Porto Santo

1964 Inauguration of Santa Catarina Airport on Madeira

1974 On 25 April the Carnation Revolution in Portugal ends the dictatorship of Estado Novo, which began in the 1930s under António de Oliveira Salazar

1976 As part of the democratisation of Portugal Madeira becomes an autonomous region

The purple flowers of the 'pride of Madeira', which is endemic to the island

helped out, some of the damage will be visible for several years to come.

Alberto João Jardim, the president of the island who has ruled Madeira for more than 30 years as head of the conservative Social Democrats, has shown that he is a man who gets things done – in difficult times as well as good ones. Where some accuse him of being a corrupt opportunist, others praise the indefatigable commitment that he devotes to the development of Madeira. Both locals and visitors benefit from the improvement of infrastructure, which has been financed largely from EU funds that Jardim untiringly applies for. In this process economic growth and protection of nature have to be reconciled. Madeira is an archipelago of contrasts: a heavy shower of rain falls – but shortly afterwards the sun is shining from a cloudless sky. Visitors see luxuriant green forests of laurel, but a dry peninsula, black lava pools and beaches of golden sand also await discovery. Come to Madeira and experience these contrasts. The local people will greet you with unforgettable warmth and the delicious specialities of the island.

1986
Portugal joins the EU

2000
Opening of the extension to Santa Catarina Airport and start of a radical enlargement of Madeira's network of fast roads

2010
In February heavy rainfall causes devastation in parts of Funchal and the south-west coast. In summer forest fires destroy areas of mountain vegetation around the Pico do Arieiro

2011
The financial crisis forces Portugal and Madeira to make savings. However, tourism booms due to the political instability in North Africa

WHAT'S HOT

1 Culinary arts in Funchal

A meeting of architects and artichokes Chefs conjure exciting dishes from familiar old ingredients, and visionary architects create the surroundings to match. The minimalist furnishings of *Fora d'Água* with lots of glass shows off the food to best advantage *(Estrada Monumental, Edifício Ocean Park, Loja 9)*. At *Xôpana* meals are served between wooden columns and massive blocks of granite *(in the Choupana Hills Resort, Travessa do Largo da Choupana)*. Foodies dine seated on furniture by Philippe Starck in the restaurant of the *CS Madeira Atlantic Resort (Estrada Monumental 175–177,* photo*)*.

Moda Madeira

2

Fashion for the night As the island gets a younger image, fashion designers set to work to create outfits suitable for clubbing. *Patrícia Pinto* likes a modern style with strong colours and see-through fabrics *(Rua Nova de São Pedro 56, Funchal)*. *Lúcia Sousa* is known for her romantic dresses *(Palácio dos Cônsules, Rua da Conceição 23, Funchal,* photo*)*. Even a football star, the fashion-conscious *Cristiano Ronaldo*, has opened a boutique in his hometown Funchal *(CR7, Rua Vale da Ajuda)*.

3 Sounds in the air

Music to love When the disparate sounds of jazz and fado come together, the result is an out-of-the-ordinary kind of music that gets under the skin. The recently established three-day *Funchal Jazz Festival* is already attracting such well-known artists as *Nnenna Freelon* (www.funchaljazzfestival.com). The restaurant *House Jazz* has made a name for itself with live jazz *(Rua dos Aranhas 16, Funchal)*. With a bit of luck the star of the scene, *Vânia Fernandes* (photo), will put in an appearance.

Where it's happening

Trendy quarter Around the Parque de Santa Catarina Funchal is getting a younger look. This was kick-started by the opening of *Dolce Vita*. This new shopping complex brought vibrant, youthful life into this district at the edge of the city centre – and a trendy quarter was born *(Centro Comercial Dolce Vita Funchal, Rua Dr. Brito Câmara 9)*. As Funchal gains a fresher image, a place with some party atmosphere is a must: the harbour is envisaged as the up-and-coming entertainment quarter. One highlight that already exists is the restaurant-cum-club *Molhe* in the old fort of *Nossa Senhora Da Conceição (Estrada da Pontinha)*. In the *FX Bar* behind the theatre live music is on the programme up to seven days a week and local musicians meet for spontaneous jam sessions *(Largo das Fontes 1– 4)*.

Visionary ecologists

Think green Ecologists who aim to save the island's ecological system for the future are initiating events like *Green Fresh Week*, when activists look out for sustainable ideas in everyday contexts like shopping expeditions or using the roads. It goes without saying that the event itself is 'green': biodiesel buses are in operation and all the merchandising items and souvenirs are produced from recycled materials *(www.greenfreshweek.com,* photo). *Nature Meetings* too have made a commitment to the principles of ecology. They educate hikers about the island's nature and help to protect the laurisilva forests *(www.walking madeira.com)*. The islanders are not short of ideas for a sustainable environment. There is a new scheme to establish an adobe-built artists' colony on the coast. The project is called *Artlantica (www.artlantica.net)*.

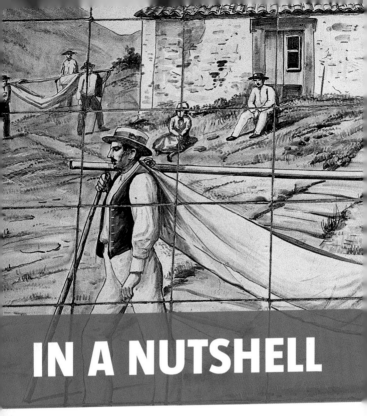

IN A NUTSHELL

A ZULEJOS

As a frieze, a medallion or a large-format picture on a wall – Portugal's decorative tiles are part of the architectural tradition on Madeira, too. The oldest of them date from the 17th century, but most were made in the early 20th century as copies. The tiles, which are often blue and white but sometimes highly colourful, shield walls from weathering and protect against heat, but at the same time they have a decorative purpose.

B RITISH HERITAGE

Britain played an important role in the history of Madeira. English merchants had great influence on the island's wine growing industry – and their families still control almost the entire production of Madeira wine. The same is true of one of the island's newspapers, as well as of many travel agents and hotels. It was a Scotsman, however, who opened the first luxury hotel: William Reid. In 1854 an Englishwoman named Elizabeth Phelps put white Madeiran embroidery on a commercial basis. And most of the holidaymakers came from Great Britain. So it's not surprising that a habit of orderly queuing, as well as the English style of bread, have become commonplace.

E MIGRATION

The phenomenon of emigration and return has been familiar on Madeira since the time of the first settlers. Many early residents who came from mainland Portugal saw the island as a stepping stone

Photo: Azulejo frieze on the Chamber of Commerce in Funchal

Quintas, levadas or azulejos – much on Madeira is distinctive and even unique

on the way to a new life in the colony of Brazil. Moorish, black African and Canarian slaves returned to their homelands when they gained their freedom. Foreign sugar merchants left Madeira when their business became unprofitable. Their workers had to look elsewhere for employment and they, too, emigrated. The same thing happened when mildew and phylloxera wiped out the island's vines almost completely in the 19th century. The preferred destinations of Madeirans looking to build a new life were, and still are today, Brazil, Venezuela, South Africa, England and the Channel Islands. Many who emigrate return to Madeira after some time and set up a small business with the money they have earned abroad. A fine-looking new house on the family land – often right next to the parents' modest home – is usually a clear sign of a returned emigrant.

ENVIRONMENT

Madeira is a relatively clean and tidy island. It is not common to find rubbish that has been tipped in levadas or by the roadside. Funchal is regularly voted the cleanest city in Portugal, and more and more Madeiran homes and hotels practise the sorting of waste. The plant for burning waste and recycling is situated on the slopes above Camacha. In the nature reserves of Madeira and Porto Santo efforts are being made to replant trees in areas where the forests were once felled. Problems are caused by plantations of eucalyptus and

Strelitzia, also known as the bird-of-paradise flower

acacia, which take a lot of water out of the soil. When heavy rainfall occurs, these trees are no longer adequately rooted on steep slopes, as happened in February 2010.

FAUNA

Madeira is not rich in wildlife, as only a few species of animals were able to reach the archipelago on their own: bats, insects and birds. Some 200 kinds of bird live on the island, including the Madeira chaffinch and the Madeira firecrest. The only species of reptile is the wall lizard. It is extremely common, and likes to eat overripe fruit in the vineyards and orchards. There is a greater variety of marine animals, from the black scabbard fish to tuna and species of squid. Whales and dolphins can sometimes be seen, and even the endangered monk seals have made a comeback. Most domestic animals – all of which were brought to the island by humans – are kept out of sight: pigs stay in their sties, and the farmers normally keep their cows and goats in traditionally built huts with pointed roofs, known as *palheiros*.

FLORA

20 per cent of the island's area is still covered with laurel forest *(laurisilva)*, which was declared a UNESCO World Heritage in 1999. This unique jungle forms the core of the Madeira nature park, which was established in 1982. In addition to several types of laurel, such as Madeiran laurel and a hardwood tree known as *vinhático*, ferns, mosses and lichens grow here in abundance. Altogether there are several dozen endemic plant species. Many walking trails are bordered by the giant dandelion and snowdrop tree. At heights above 1200 m types of heather and tree heath are dominant, with patches of lemon yellow from the Madeira violet and the white flowers of saxifrage. On a few stretches of rocky coast the original lowland flora can still be found. Otherwise the lush green of Madeira is mainly man-made, from the banana terraces and groves of eucalyptus or acacia to the extensive growths of cactus and tropical or subtropical gardens. All year round there is something in bloom: in spring, for example, hydrangeas, rhododendrons and the Jerusalem cherry, or the delicate mauve of the jacaranda tree. In summer lilies of the Nile (agapanthus), Pride of Madeira, frangipani (Plumeria) and dragon trees are in flower. In autumn belladonna lilies open their buds, kapok trees blossom and begonias are in bloom. In winter callas, camellias and large poinsettia bushes de-

light the eye, and all year round hibiscus, bougainvillea, strelitzia, anthuriums and African tulip trees ensure a blaze of colour.

FRUIT

Thanks to several centuries of intensive cultivation and excellent climatic conditions, Madeira has become a true Garden of Eden. From apples to exotic fruit, almost everything thrives on the island: apricots, bananas, cherries, mangoes, passion fruit, melons, oranges, papayas, pineapples and plums, as well as grapes for eating (on Porto Santo) and cherimoyas. Add to that guavas, figs, and less-known varieties such as the *nêspera* (a kind of loquat), *pitanga* (Surinam cherry) and *aração* (rose apple). The sweet-sour tamarillo or tree tomato (also called *tomate inglês*) is something between a fruit and a vegetable. *Licor de maracujá* syrup and a lemonade-like drink are made from passion fruit.

LEVADAS

Soon after the island was discovered, slaves made the first artificial channels in order to conduct water from distant springs to the sugar-cane plantations. In the 19th century, when the cultivation of sugar cane was revived, the historic system of water channels was revitalised and extended. As the population had increased tenfold in the intervening centuries, it was no longer enough simply to divert spring water on the south side of the island. For the irrigation of many areas of agricultural land the water was now channelled from the rainier north side to the plantations in the south, at the cost of great effort and using tunnels in places. Most of the levada network, which now has a length of more than 2000 km (1.250 mi), was created in the 20th century. In building it, Salazar's government also had a mind to generating power: about ten per cent of the electric-

Eucalyptus and laurel forest on the Levada da Ribeira da Janela

ity needed on the island today comes from hydroelectric plants that are connected to levadas. These narrow channels, once the property of the big landowners, now mainly belong to the state. Every farmer buys a certain quantity of water each year from the state. A *levadeiro* monitors the distribution and is also responsible for maintaining the watercourses. Visitors to Madeira can use most of the paths made by the *levadeiros* for maintenance. They provide wonderful short walks and longer hikes.

MADEIRA WINE

The secret of this dessert wine, which contains about 20 per cent alcohol, is to be found in the addition of brandy, which stops the fermentation process, and in the subsequent heating of the liquid. Originally, Madeira wine was warmed by natural means: the sun shone for years on oak barrels filled with maturing wine, which were not stored in wine cellars but in wine lofts. Nowadays almost all producers resort to technical aids, and the desired conditions are achieved rapidly – sometimes too rapidly – using steel tanks and spiral water tubes. Madeira wine is made from four traditional types of fine grape: Sercial (dry), Verdelho (medium dry), Boal (medium sweet) and Malvasia (sweet). The older the Madeira, the more rounded the taste and the more impressive the price.

MANUELINE STYLE

King Manuel I, who reigned in Portugal from 1495 to 1521, was also known as Manuel the Fortunate, because under his rule, thanks to the success of Vasco da Gama and other navigators in undertaking voyages of exploration and conquest, Portugal enjoyed its golden age of global renown and prosperity. King Manuel employed the wealth that flowed in from Portuguese supremacy on the seas to build magnificent monasteries, churches, towers and palaces, which are opulently adorned with maritime decorative features. On Madeira, too, many buildings, especially churches and chapels can be seen decorated with the typical symbols of the Manueline style: nautical rope in stone, algae and corals encrusting portals, and balustrades adorned with the eight-pointed cross of the Military Order of Christ. The symbol of Henry the Navigator is much in evidence: it is an armillary sphere, an instrument used in navigation.

PEOPLE

The people of Madeira have a quiet air that is not so easily ruffled. Even in an absolute emergency during the catastrophic storms in February 2010 they kept their calm and cleaned up the mess. Most of the front gardens on the island also have a well-kept appearance. How things look behind the façade, however, is something that visitors rarely get to see: although Madeirans are very warm-hearted and extremely hospitable towards members of the family, it is not usual to let strangers into the house. Most celebrations are held out of doors anyway: at street parties and village festivals, with wine, skewers of succulent meat and traditional music – and often arm in arm with the president of the island, Alberto João Jardim, who has the common touch. Jardim, who seems immune to electoral defeat, is surpassed in fame by only one native of Madeira: Cristiano Ronaldo, one of the world's best footballers, who was born in 1985 in humble circumstances and thrills his compatriots on Madeira with every goal he scores and every visit he pays to his home.

PORTUGAL

On 25 April 1974 the peaceful Carnation Revolution brought an end to dictatorship in Portugal, which had begun in the early 1930s under António de Oliveira Salazar. During the *Estado Novo* the dictator never showed much interest in the Portuguese Atlantic islands and neglected investments in their development. When democracy was introduced, in 1976 Madeira received special status as an autonomous region, ruled by its own president who is elected by the people of the island. In internal affairs, Madeira thus gained a degree of independence. However, the government in Lisbon makes use of its powers to control the island parliament, and important decisions are taken 'on the continent', as the Madeirans put it. They keep a palpable emotional distance to their brothers and sisters *do continente,* but for lack of opportunities on the island many young people move to Lisbon, Porto or Coimbra to study or train for work.

ing restored and used as hotels, the seats of institutions or museums. They make a pleasing contrast to the wave of concrete manifested in the island's construction boom, which was fuelled for a long time by money from the EU.

QUINTAS

Hundreds of these country seats were once scattered all over the island. Most of them date back to the 18th and

SUGAR CANE

Prince Henry the Navigator brought sugar cane from Sicily to Madeira in the early 15th century. The first sugar mill

The machines in the sugar-cane factory in Calheta are still driven by steam power

19th centuries, when the wine trade flourished and great numbers of British merchants settled on Madeira. They commissioned architects from across the world to carry out the work following the latest stylistic trends, and employed gardeners to create luxuriant landscapes with exotic plants around their imposing residences. From the mid-20th century onwards property speculation and new buildings spelled the end for many quintas. Today this exquisite architectural heritage is appreciated again. Historic houses are be-

went into operation in 1452, and by 1500 Madeira was supplying all of Europe with 'white gold'. The sugar barons took works of art in exchange for their goods – which is why Madeira has a fine collection of Flemish paintings of the 15th and 16th centuries. Faced with increasing competition from South America, Madeiran planters abandoned the large-scale cultivation of sugar cane, but the coat of arms of Funchal shows how important this trade once was: it displays five sugarloaves.

FOOD & DRINK

Lovers of sweet wine lick their lips straight away when they hear the name Madeira: the island's wine makes a wonderful aperitif or after-dinner drink. A typical Madeiran meal usually starts with soup, which is followed by a hearty helping of the main course.

In the island's traditional peasant cooking, 'good' is synonymous with 'plenty'. With a little luck you will find tasty, down-to-earth specialities such as wheat soup or INSIDER TIP watercress soup *(sopa de trigo, sopa de agriões)*, tripe stew *(dobrada)*, boiled kid *(cabrito)* and pork with wine and garlic *carne vinho e alhos* in a village pub. The cooks in tourist hotels and restaurants stick to standard international fare, while French, Far Eastern and crossover cuisine are the main styles in

gourmet restaurants. A good chef is also able to conjure surprising culinary treats from staples like *bacalhau* (dried cod). The twin pillars of the island's food, however, are *espada* and *espetada* – scabbard fish and skewered beef. Another popular main course is tuna *(atum)*, often served in a strong onion dip. Swordfish *(espadarte)*, grouper *(garoupa)*, red snapper *(pargo)*, gilthead bream *(dourada)*, parrotfish *(bodião)* and *cavaco*, a kind of langoustine, often also feature on the menu. *Camarões* (shrimps) and INSIDER TIP *caramujos* (sea snails) are sometimes advertised on a notice on the door of little country bars as the day's speciality. Almost all restaurants serve limpets *(lapas)*. Fresh mountain trout *(trutas)* make a delicious change from

Rustic and plentiful – Madeiran cooking still revolves around down-to-earth dishes such as espada and espetada

sea fish. They are farmed in Ribeiro Frio. Madeirans prefer *frango* and *bife* – chicken and beefsteak – to fish, which is fairly expensive. At celebrations it is usual for dozens of whole chickens to be sizzling on the grill as an alternative to *espetada*. Unfortunately almost all the chickens come from intensive farming. Madeirans often eat their beefsteak in the form of sandwiches. A great deal of beef is imported – and the same is true of pork.

The main supplement to meat is potatoes, boiled or as French fries. Some-

times sweet potatoes baked in their skins *(batata doce)* or *milho frito* also appear on the menu. The latter is maize polenta, seasoned with herbs and diced. *Inhame* is a member of the yam family. With a bit of luck you will be served this boiled root, which has a distinctive taste, as an accompaniment to meat dishes. As in the past this plant was often the only source of nourishment in times of hunger, it is still regarded as food for the poor and turns up more often in home cooking than on the menus of high-class res-

LOCAL SPECIALITIES

▶ **açorda** – clear, hearty bread soup with garlic and egg, ideally served in a big bowl from which guests can help themselves repeatedly

▶ **arroz de marisco** – a juicy stew made from rice, fish and other seafood, often garnished with prawns and large mussels, and seasoned with fresh coriander. Mostly available as a dish for two people, sometimes with spaghetti instead of rice *(esparguete de marisco)*

▶ **bolo do caco** – a round, flat white loaf, originally made from sweet potatoes but nowadays mainly from flour, which is browned on hot iron hobs

▶ **bolo de mel** – a dark, spiced cake containing sugar-cane syrup (photo right)

▶ **caldeirada** – thick, spicy fish stew

▶ **carne vinho e alhos** – diced pork, marinated for a long time in wine and vinegar with garlic and bay leaf or fennel, then braised

▶ **castanhetas** – small fish like anchovies, fried and tossed in garlic oil

▶ **espada** – the black scabbard fish features on the menu almost everywhere, often filleted and served with banana; however the locals also cook this fish with wine and garlic

▶ **espetada** – the island's national dish. Traditionally the beef is freshly diced, rolled in coarse-grained bay-leaf salt and stuck on a skewer of laurel wood to sizzle over open coals until the meat is ready to eat

▶ **lapas grelhadas** – limpets harvested fresh from coastal rocks are extremely tasty. They are prepared by cooking them with garlic butter and lemon juice on a hot metal platter from which they are then eaten (photo left)

▶ **poncha** – the fishermen of Câmara de Lobos claim to be the inventors of this drink made from mixing clear sugar-cane spirit with lemon juice and honey

▶ **prego (no prato)** – 'nail (on the plate)' is the literal translation of the name for this combination of a thin piece of fried beef with a lettuce leaf and tomato. This healthy trio of ingredients is popular as a sandwich between two halves of a roll

▶ **tremoços** – preserved salty lupin seeds, served as an alternative to chicken stomachs or chopped pig's ears as a nibble with beer *(dentinhos)*

taurants. When it comes to vegetables, carrots and beans from the island's gardens are much in evidence; sometimes a restaurant owner dishes up *pimpinela* (chayote, a kind of pale green gourd), which is often eaten at home. Many other types of vegetable are imported, often from Africa.

Beer, by contrast, is normally made locally. The leading brand on Madeira is Coral. If you want beer on draught, ask for an *imperial*. It is often mixed with lemonade to make *shandy*. The island's table wine, which enthusiastic wine makers have been producing for about ten years now, is still drunk relatively little, and wines brought in from Portugal are more common.

At festivals local wines – light-heartedly known on Madeira as *café de setembro*, September coffee – come into their own. They are usually served from plastic jugs, are rarely more than a year old and have been made privately in the traditional way. Their taste is somewhat between earthy and sour, which is why the Madeirans tend to mix them with lemonade. In Santo da Serra and Camacha there is another traditional mixed drink: *cidra*, i.e. cider, to which sugar or honey is added.

Quer sobremesa? There's no escaping the question about dessert, and on Madeira the answer is generally yes. Home-made cakes *(bolos)*, passion-fruit pudding, crème caramel or fresh fruit are the usual choices.

After a meal Madeirans always order coffee. If they like it small and black, they order a *bica* (espresso) or a *bica curta* (the even stronger version). If they prefer to dilute their coffee with a little milk, they ask for a *garoto*. A larger milky coffee is known as a *chinesa*.

A brew made from lemon rind and hot water is called *chá de limão* on the island.

This drink, and coffee too, are available as *pingado* – with a shot of spirits, usually whisky.

When it's time to pay the bill, 'one for all' is the guiding principle. It is not normal for each guest to pay separately: either the guests then divide the amount amongst themselves, or those who don't pay will take their turn next time the

Refreshing and delicious: passion-fruit drink

group eats out. If nevertheless you do wish to pay separately, when asking the waiter to bring the bill you should make the request with these words: *A conta em separado, se faz favor.*

The bill often includes an item called *couverts.* These appetisers consist only of bread and butter, or sometimes olives too, in simple *tascas*, while in better-class restaurants there might be plates with shrimps, smoked ham or a special cheese. If guests sample something from these plates, which are generously placed on the table in welcome, they will appear later on the bill, usually at a steep price. If you don't want these hors d'oeuvres, the best thing to do is hand them back to the waiter straight away.

SHOPPING

Madeira wine is probably the best-known souvenir from the island. However, there are other attractive products that will remind you of Madeira and its charming atmosphere when you are back home. Why not buy some exotic fruit, honey (often sold in prettily decorated jars), a *bolo de mel* (cake ideally bought from the local baker), chirimoya or passion-fruit liqueur, or even the island's sugar-cane spirit, *aguardente de cana*?

Hand-made traditional boots or sandals (or maybe a pair of elegant Portuguese designer shoes from one of the boutiques in Funchal) also make a great souvenir. The pointed caps with earflaps and a bobble, which are knitted from coarse wool and still used by many men in country areas as protection against wind and cold, are amusing and useful at the same time. *Brinquinhos*, traditional rattle instruments with colourful wooden figures that look like a Turkish crescent, evoke images of merry folk festivals.

FLOWERS

Strelitzias, proteas, orchids and many other exotic plants are grown on the 'island of flowers' in a number of nurseries and in the Jardim Botânico, and can be purchased or ordered there directly. Retailers of quality, including some small shops, will pack these fragile wares for you without additional charge so that they arrive home with you undamaged. A wide selection of flower bulbs, agapanthus for example, are on sale in the market hall in Funchal. *Jardim Botânico da Madeira (Caminho do Meio, Bom Sucesso, Funchal, www.madeirabotanicalgarden. com); Jardim Quinta da Boa Vista (Rua do Lombo da Boa Vista, Funchal, only orchids); A Rosa (Rua Imperatriz D. Amélia 126, Funchal)*

BASKETRY

There is not yet a seal of quality for basketwork as there is for embroidery, so not every product was truly made on Madeira. To be sure of getting the genuine article, the best course of action is to go to the basket weaver's studio, or place your trust in one of the cooperatives, for example at *Café Relógio* in Camacha. The assortment of basketwork is wide – it ranges from basket bottles to garden seats. Bulky items can be shipped for you. The sales outlet of the cooperatives in Funchal is: *Vimescope, Rua da Carreira 102*

Delicate, floral and liquid products – embroidery, flowers and Madeira wine are some of the most popular souvenirs

MADEIRA EMBROIDERY

Authentic Madeira embroideries *(bordados)* are appreciated by political leaders and those who dictate the fashion world in equal measure. A British lady was responsible for raising the standards in a traditional craft practised by the wives of fishermen and turning it into a flourishing industry. Nowadays only a few *bordadeiras* are left to carry out this badly paid embroidery work on a professional basis – and that means high prices. Vendors are therefore highly tempted to add cheap, imported, machine-produced goods to their assortment, so when buying look out for the **INSIDER TIP** seal of quality of the IVBAM (Instituto do Vinho, do Bordado e do Artesanato da Madeira), which also runs a fashion and design centre.

MADEIRA WINE

When buying Madeira wine, bear in mind the following rule of thumb: five years is the minimum period of maturing to achieve good quality. A bottle of fine old Madeira wine can then cost as much as an evening meal. In compensation the wine will keep for several months, even after the bottle is opened. *Artur de Barros e Sousa*, a family-run company, is the only one on the island that still produces according to the traditional method: in wooden barrels and without heat from artificial sources. The result is a small selection of extremely fine wines. *Rua dos Ferreiros 109, Funchal, www.vinhosmadeira.com*

PERFUME & COSMETICS

One of the newest business ideas on Madeira is the production of perfume, especially from orchids and strelitzias, and the manufacture of **INSIDER TIP** natural cosmetics from aloe vera. The creams and ointments made in Caniçal to soothe sunburn, torn muscles or arthritis are becoming popular purchases. They can be found in well-stocked souvenir shops, pharmacies and health-food stores.

THE PERFECT ROUTE

FROM FUNCHAL TO THE MOUNTAINS

The perfect route starts in ① *Funchal* → p. 32, the fashionable and attractive capital of the island. From here drive to ② *Monte* → p. 47, a place of pilgrimage famous for its basket sled trips and tropical park (photo left), and up into Madeira's rugged mountain country. After a detour to ③ *Pico do Arieiro* → p. 90 for a view of the jagged mountain peaks of the island, follow the winding road down again towards the north coast. The attractions in ④ *Ribeiro Frio* → p. 73 are plump trout and lush laurel forest, which you can explore on a short walk to the ☙ Balcões viewing point.

VILLAGES IN THE NORTH

⑤ *Santana* → p. 63 is famous for its colourful thatched houses and excellent home cooking. Why not try a bowl of wheat soup (*sopa de trigo*) here? The bendy coast road to the west, which has not yet all been improved by building tunnels, leads through idyllic little villages like ⑥ *São Jorge* → p. 66, Arco de São Jorge and Ponta Delgada. In ⑦ *São Vicente* → p. 67 the church is hidden behind a rock, and it is well worth visiting the centre of the little town. If you have always wanted to see a volcano from the inside, then the place to stop is Grutas de São Vicente, where unique views of what lies within Madeira can be had.

ALONG THE NORTH COAST

Continue on the north coast road to Porto Moniz. In some places the road goes through modern tunnels, as the old coast road became too dangerous. Don't forget to make a stop at the ☙ viewing point named ⑧ *Véu da Noiva* → p. 69 in order to enjoy the sight of the sheer cliff walls and their waterfalls evoking a bride's veil. In ⑨ *Porto Moniz* → p. 61 the highlights are a swim in the seawater rock pools formed from the lava and a visit to the aquarium in the old fort. This fishing port is an excellent place to try grilled limpets (*lapas grelhadas*) as well as freshly caught fish.

ACROSS THE HIGHLANDS

The ⑩ *Paúl da Serra* → p. 55 plateau is a fine place for hiking when the weather is good. It is the starting point for many routes around Rabaçal, one of the island's best areas for walkers. The road across

Enjoy the many facets of Madeira on this drive, which takes you into the mountains, then along the north coast and back to the south

the plateau, straight as a die in places, leads down to the ⑪ *Encumeada Pass* → p. 58. With a little luck you will get a view of the north and south coasts at the same time from here, before continuing through the ⑫ *Serra de Água* → p. 59 valley back to the south coast. This is one of the best places to try a drink of *poncha* – get your designated driver to stop at a poncha bar by the wayside!

THE SUNNY SOUTH

In ⑬ *Ribeira Brava* → p. 57, once a flourishing trade centre, take a stroll along the sea promenade and a look at the Ethnographic Museum. A panoramic lift takes you down to remote ⑭ *Fajã dos Padres* → p. 44, where you can experience lunch and real solitude amongst the exotic fruits that are cultivated there. The reward for making a detour to 🔆 ⑮ *Cabo Girão* → p. 44, one of the world's tallest cliffs, is a magnificent view out to the Atlantic and as far as the Bay of Funchal. In the fishing village of ⑯ *Câmara de Lobos* → p. 44 (photo right) Winston Churchill once painted the lively harbour scene with picturesque houses framed by rocks.

VALLEY OF THE NUNS

Before returning to Funchal, be sure to take a trip to the 'valley of nuns', ⑰ *Curral das Freiras* → p. 46, with its specialities made from chestnuts. The view from the 🔆 viewpoint of ⑱ *Eira do Serrado* → p. 46 alone makes it worth driving this winding road: the village is surrounded on all sides by spectacular mountain slopes.

95 miles. Driving time 4–5 hours. Detailed map of the route on the back cover, in the road atlas and the pull-out map.

FUNCHAL

 **MAP INSIDE THE BACK COVER**
'Little Lisbon' was the name given to
Funchal (130–131 A–D 5–6) *(⌘ K–M 7–8)*
in the 16th century by Italian navigators
– only a few years after João Zarco, the
discoverer of the island, transferred his
residence from Câmara de Lobos to this
bay, which was overgrown with wild fennel (funcho).

The little town prospered through the
export of sugar. Elegant buildings soon
stood between the banks of the rivers
that run into the sea here.

Today about 132,000 people, i.e. more
than half of all Madeirans, live in Funchal.
Like an amphitheatre from ancient times,
the city has spread up the slopes of the
mountains that surround it. Expanding to
the southwest with the construction of a

coastal strip, a hotel quarter that gained a
lovely green promenade next to the ocean,
it will soon have covered the last remain-

> **CITY** **WHERE TO START?**
> **Old quarter:** with its narrow
> alleys, the old quarter of Funchal
> (*zona velha*) is a good choice to
> start a visit. On the western edge
> of this, the oldest district of the city,
> you can park in the Almirante Reis
> garage *(Rua Dom Carlos I)*. The
> central bus station and terminus
> of the cable car to Monte are also
> here. The market hall *(Mercado dos
> Lavradores)* and the São Tiago fort
> are very close by.

Photo: Palm garden in the hotel zone

Everyone comes to the 'bay of fennel' –
Funchal is not only the capital, but also the
vibrant tourist centre of the island

ing banana fields. Towards the east it will
not be long before Funchal has merged
with the neighbouring town of Caniço.
The historic city centre and the old, heav-
ily restored fishermen's quarter *(zona velha)* can easily be explored on foot. To get
a first impression, the tour in an open-
top double-decker bus with commentary
(1 hour, in English and other languages)
is recommended *(Carristur | 12 euros |
ticket valid 24 hours | information and
starting point: Avenida do Mar, opposite
the Casa do Turista | www.carristur.pt)*.

AVENIDA ARRIAGA

The city's number one street for prom-
enading, adorned with jacaranda trees,
terminates at the cathedral and *Praça do
Infante* with a monument to Henry the
Navigator. The avenue is particularly pretty in late spring when the trees unfold
their purple blossom. It is fringed by the
Teatro Municipal Baltazar Dias, the Neo-
classical municipal theatre built in the
early 20th century, the former Chamber

of Commerce with its traditional azulejo pictures and the little *Jardim Municipal*. The ruins of a Franciscan monastery once has been converted into a café. On the side of the road facing the city stands the Fortaleza de São Lourenço, and

A promenade beneath jacaranda trees: Avenida Arriaga in Funchal

stood where the massive trees of this municipal park now grow. Remains of the monastery buildings can be found inside the *Adegas de São Francisco*, the seat of the *Madeira Wine Company* (Mon–Fri 10am–6pm, Sat 10am–1pm | tour with wine tasting 5 euros | Av. Arriaga 28 | www.madeirawinecompany.com).

AVENIDA DO MAR
'Ocean Avenue' is both the main traffic artery and a place to take a stroll. Along the Avenida are many bus stops, and the green harbour promenade runs along the Atlantic side. By day and in the evening its cafés and restaurant draw in local people. Huge cruise ships anchor by the quay, yachts bob to and fro on the waves; the Vagrant, once the Beatles' yacht, is on dry land today and

further east, the old customs house *Alfândega Velha* is now the seat of the island parliament.

CASA MUSEU FREDERICO DE FREITAS
This 17th-century villa is filled with valuable furniture, old azulejos, religious and Chinese art. Its former owner drew and painted views of his Madeiran homeland. *Closed Sun/Mon | admission 2.50 euros | Calçada de Santa Clara 7*

CONVENTO DE SANTA CLARA
This nunnery built in the late 15th century for the Order of St Clare, or Poor Clares, today harbours a nursery school. The walls of the church are completely covered in early 17th-century azulejos. Inside the church are the tombs of the two daughters of João Zarco and, it is said,

the grave of Zarco himself. One of the friendly Franciscan sisters who run the convent today tells fascinating stories from the history of the nunnery as part of a tour of the historic buildings (tour in English). *Sun closed | admission 2 euros | Calçada de Santa Clara 15*

FORTALEZA DE SÃO LOURENÇO

The fort is part of a ring of fortifications that surrounded Funchal from the 17th to the 19th century. It is now in government hands as the residence of both the Minister of the Republic and the military commander. However, visitors are allowed inside at certain times *(Wed 10am, Fri 3pm, Sat 11am)*, and by appointment *(tel. 2 91 20 25 30). Free admission | entrance: Av. Zarco*

FORTE DE SÃO TIAGO

Construction of this fortress on the eastern edge of the bay began in 1614, and further buildings were added in the 18th century. Flights of steps lead up to the ☆ roof terrace, where visitors have a fine panoramic view. On the upper floors the *Museu de Arte Contemporânea* (Museum of Contemporary Art) displays works by Portuguese artists from the 1960s to the present day. *Sun closed | admission 2.50 euros | Rua Portão de São Tiago*

FORTALEZA DO PICO DE SÃO JOÃO ☆

High up on the 111-metre Pico dos Frias, this fort, which was built early in the 17th century under Spanish rule, commands INSIDER TIP ▶ one of the best views of the city centre of Funchal. Once a gunpowder magazine for the forts of the island, it is now used by the navy as a communications centre. The masts and antennas installed there have led locals to call the hill ‚Pico Rádio‘. *Daily 9am–6pm | free admission | Rua do Castelo*

INSIDER TIP ▶ **IGREJA DO SOCORRO**

In fulfilment of a vow, the inhabitants of Funchal built a pilgrimage chapel here after an outbreak of plague in the early 16th century. Two hundred years later, the present ‘Church of Succour’ was erected. Its façade shows the Baroque style in a purer form than any other church on Madeira. *Largo do Socorro*

CATHEDRAL (SÉ)

King Manuel I ordered the construction of Funchal's leading place of worship. The church was completed between 1485 and 1514, and is one of the city's few sur

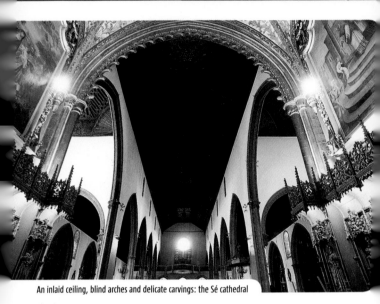
An inlaid ceiling, blind arches and delicate carvings: the Sé cathedral

viving examples of the Manueline architectural style. Its name derives from *sede do bispo*, the seat or throne of the bishop. Its steeple is clad in multi-coloured roof tiles, while in the plain stone-built façade a majestic Gothic doorway catches the eye. The architecture at the eastern end of the church with the apse is more playful: turrets twist like screws, and the balustrade is elaborately decorated. The finest feature inside is the 16th-century wooden roof in the Mudéjar style, which is inlaid with ivory. *Largo da Sé*

MADEIRA STORY CENTRE ●

This interactive museum is situated at the heart of the *zona velha,* Funchal's old quarter. It takes visitors on a virtual journey back to the beginnings of Madeira, shows them how the island developed and gets them involved in the most important historical events on the archipelago. An interesting presentation, not only for children! The museum

shop sells tasteful souvenirs, from flower bulbs to thermos flasks. *Daily | admission 9.60 euros | Rua D. Carlos 27–29 | www. storycentre.com*

MERCADO DOS LAVRADORES ★ ●

Built in 1941, and clearly harking back to the Art Deco style, the 'workers' market' has beautiful, large-format azulejo pictures at the entrance, but the real attraction is the abundance of products, including wonderful displays of fruit and vegetables. Butchers' stalls surround the courtyard on the ground floor, and other shops sell wine, basketware and souvenirs, for example the traditional Madeira boots. Steps lead from the courtyard down to the fish hall. In the café on the roof terrace, vendors and shoppers can relax in wicker chairs to recover from all the hard work of buying and selling over a cup of coffee. *Mon–Fri 7am–8pm, Sat 7am–2pm | Rua Latino Coelho*

MUSEU DE ARTE SACRA

Located in what was once the bishop's palace, the Museum of Religious Art houses a major collection of Flemish paintings from the 16th to 18th centuries, statues of saints from the same period and decorative items from churches. *Closed Sun pm, Mon | admission 3 euros | Rua do Bispo 21 | www.museuartesacrafunchal.org*

MUSEU HISTÓRIA NATURAL

Stuffed mammals and birds in the Natural History Museum present the fauna of Madeira. Other exhibits are devoted to the flora and geology of the island, and the aquarium shows its marine life. *Mon closed | admission 3.55 euros, Sun free | Rua da Mouraria 31*

NÚCLEO MUSEOLÓGICO DA CIDADE DO AÇÚCAR

In the former residence of the Flemish sugar baron João Esmeraldo, prints, paintings and documents tell the story of sugar manufacture on Madeira and its cultural and artistic consequences. *Closed Sat/Sun | admission 2 euros | Praça Colombo 5*

INSIDER TIP NÚCLEO MUSEOLÓGICO DO I.V.B.A.M

The museum of embroidery is part of the state institute for wine, embroidery and crafts (IVBAM). The exhibition displays precious embroidery work from the 19th century and Art Nouveau period, including tapestries. In some rooms of the museum these works of art are presented along with typical period furnishings and costumes. *Closed Sat/Sun | admission 2 euros | Rua Visconde de Anadia 44*

PARQUE DE SANTA CATARINA

High above the harbour, this park extends across broad slopes with exotic trees, flowerbeds and three striking buildings. The one closest to the city centre is the Baroque *Capela de Santa Catarina*, which dates from the late 15th century. To the west of the lake, the pink walls of the *Quinta Vigia* shimmer through the dense vegetation. This historic 17th-century residence is the office and guesthouse for the president of the regional government. It is not possible to visit the inside of the quinta, but its lovely park is open to the public. A few paces further in the direction of the hotel zone stands Funchal's *Casino*. Oscar Niemeyer, architect of the modern city of Brasília, built it in the 1970s, along with the Pestana Casino Park Hotel, in the shape of a crown of thorns. In front of this curved building, which is supported on stilts, a bronze statue serves as a reminder that Empress Elisabeth of Austria stayed on this site in 1860–61. The quinta in which she resided was demolished to build the casino. *Pestana Casino Park Hotel Av. do Infante*

PHOTOGRAPHIA MUSEU VICENTES ★

Photographer Vicente Gomes da Silva (1827–1906) opened Portugal's first photo studio in 1846 in Funchal. As he was the island's most renowned photographer, many famous people posed in front of his camera during their stay on Madeira. In the old rooms of the studio behind the charming patio visitors can still admire the original equipment, including historic cameras, the darkroom, as well as costumes and stage sets for taking portraits. The old black-and-white prints from the large photographic archive assembled by four generations of Vicentes, who ran the business until the end of the 1970s, are even more interesting. The photos are a documentation of Madeira as it was in the 19th and 20th centuries, showing eminent residents and visitors to the island. *Closed Sat/Sun | admission 2.50 euros | Rua Carreira 43*

PRAÇA DO MUNICÍPIO

The square with its black-and-white paving is bordered by three of Funchal's significant historic buildings. At the end of the square is the former town residence of the Counts of Carvalhal. Since the late 19th century this Baroque palace with its magnificent, azulejo-adorned courtyard

The cable car up to Monte

has been the home of Funchal *city hall*. The northwest side of the square is dominated by what used to be a Jesuit college and is now the *University* of Madeira. An impressive church, the *Igreja do Colégio*, forms part of the complex. Opposite the church, the *Bishop's Palace* now houses the Museum of Religious Art.

QUINTA DAS CRUZES

The home of João Zarco is said to have occupied this site. Today's residence, however, dates from the 18th century and is a museum demonstrating the lifestyle of rich citizens of Madeira in the past. Sometimes INSIDER TIP concerts of classical music are held here. The quinta lies within an archaeological park with exotic plants and stone Manueline windows, as well as a fragment of the 15th-century pillory *(pelourinho)* of Funchal. *Closed Mon | admission 2.50 euros, Sun and garden free | Calçada do Pico 1*

SANTA MARIA QUARTER (ZONA VELHA)

The original settlement of Funchal lay between the banks of the João Gomes river and the fort of São Tiago. In the middle of the old quarter stands the *Capela do Corpo Santo*, a brotherhood chapel built by fishermen in the Manueline period. Despite continuing restoration, a touch of the original atmosphere can still be felt in the alleyways. Alongside trendy boutiques some quaint corner shops and traditional craft shops remain in the old buildings, which for the most part date from the 18th and 19th centuries, when they replaced the original wood-built houses. In the evenings there's a lot going on here, as fado taverns, restaurants and bars (some of them with persistent touts outside) have moved into the former fishermen's homes. Passing over the roofs are the cabins of the modern ★ ☆ *cable car*, which runs from the terminus in the park of Almirante Reis up to Monte (at an altitude of 560 m). This gentle ride (15 min) provides wonderful panoramic views of Funchal and the valley of the Ribeira de João Gomes – and is an opportunity to look down on the residents' roof terraces. *Teleféricos da Madeira | daily 10am–6pm | 10 euros one way, 15 euros return | www. madeiracablecar.com*

INSIDER TIP ACENDER AROMAS CAFÉ

Tiny shop and coffee bar that puts choco-
holics in temptation's way. *Corner of Rua
do Conselheiro/Av. Arriaga* | *Budget*

ADEGA A CUBA

Hearty meals at reasonable prices in
a cosy wine bar atmosphere in the
heart of the city. *Rua do Bispo 28* | *tel.
2 91 22 09 86* | *Budget–Moderate*

BIO-LOGOS ☺

Vegetarian and macrobiotic meals made
from organically grown ingredients
are the speciality of this restaurant. A
little shop for organic products is at-
tached. *Rua Nova de São Pedro 34* | *tel.
2 91 23 68 68* | *Moderate*

INSIDER TIP DOCA DO CAVACAS

A fish restaurant by the sea – just the
way it's supposed to be, and particularly
romantic at sunset. Excellent fish and
seafood dishes at reasonable prices. The
Poças do Gomes natural swimming pools
located below the restaurant are also
worth a visit. *Estrada Monumental/Ponta
da Cruz* | *tel. 2 91 76 20 57* | *Moderate*

DOM PEPE

An ambitious and refined version of
Madeiran and Portuguese traditional
cuisine with the standards of service of
a high-class restaurant. Excellent wine
list. *Rua da Levada dos Barreiros* | *tel.
2 91 76 32 40* | *Expensive*

GOLDEN GATE GRAND CAFÉ

The coffee house in Funchal: this is
the place to meet for a *bica* in the Art
Nouveau café, or enjoy the midday set
menu with an international flavour. Also
excellent for reading newspapers (international newspapers are provided) or
people-watching on Avenida Arriaga! *Av.
Arriaga 29* | *tel. 2 91 23 43 83* | *Moderate*

GRAND CAFÉ COLUMBUS

A wide selection of snacks, sandwiches, omelettes, also soups, salads and
pasta. *Av. do Mar e das Comunidades
Madeirenses 36* | *tel. 2 91 24 21 70* | *www.
grandcafecolumbus.com* | *Budget–Mod-
erate*

INSIDER TIP O REGIONAL

From the garlic bread with home-made
dips to the luscious seafood stew with
spaghetti, the dishes served here delight the palate, and the waiters with
their traditional colourful waistcoats
are helpful and warm-hearted. *Rua de
D. Carlos I 54* | *tel. 2 91 23 29 56* | *Moder-
ate–Expensive*

LOW BUDGET

▶ All the *museums* in Funchal open
without charge on 18 May (world
museum day) and 27 September
(world tourism day). The *Jardim
Botânico* offers free admission on
30 April (its anniversary) and on 21
March (world forest day).

▶ Many restaurants in Funchal serve
a *dish of the day (prato do dia)*, usually at a price well below 8 euros
– and often that includes soup and
a drink.

▶ While most of the large gardens
charge admission, some parks are
free: *Santa Catarina* and *Jardim Municipal* parks, the *Jardim Panorâmico*
in the hotel zone and the *Parque
Municipal do Monte*. The plants are
marked with their names, and can
be enjoyed while strolling on shady
paths.

RESTAURANTE DO FORTE
High-class creations using local and Portuguese produce such as scabbard fish and salmon with spinach, in an elegant pavilion by the ● São Tiago fort. *Rua Portão São Tiago | tel. 2 91 215 5 80 | www.restaurantedoforte.com.pt | Expensive*

RISO ✂
Everything revolves around rice here. Portuguese classics are combined with the tastes of Asia, and are served in imaginative variations from crispy to sweet. A wonderful terrace on the cliffs. *Rua de Santa Maria 274 | tel. 2 91 28 03 60 | Moderate–Expensive*

SHOPPING

CASA DO TURISTA ●
This place may sound very commercial, but what lies behind the name almost amounts to a small crafts museum: Madeira embroidery and other craft products are presented in lovingly decorated rooms. Alongside antique furniture and old-fashioned flower arrangements, the hand-embroidered tablecloths really come into their own. Visitors are cordially invited inside just to admire the expensive artefacts, even if they don't intend to buy. *Rua do Conselheiro José Silvestre Ribeiro 2*

FÁBRICA SANTO ANTÓNIO
Home-made confectionery, jams, sorbets and biscuits in a historic shop. *Travessa do Forno 27/29*

MADEIRA SHOPPING ✂
Madeira's largest shopping centre, which lies above Funchal, consists of over 100 shops, seven cinema screens, almost 20 restaurants and cafés and a *hipermercado* – with a fantastic view of the sea thrown in. *Sun–Thu 10am–11pm, Fri/Sat 10am–midnight | Caminho de Santa Quitéria 45 | Santo António | www.madeirashopping.pt*

MERCADO DA AGRICULTURA BIOLÓGICA ☺
Every Wednesday Madeira's organic farmers sell their products next to the São Lourenço fort. *Largo da Restauração*

BEACHES & SPORTS

BEACHES
Funchal does not have a white beach for sunbathers like Calheta and Machico, but there are some attractive ways to get into the sea – *via steps on the rocky coast or across the pebbles of a beach. Praia Formosa* in the west of Funchal, much loved by young locals, is one such pebbly beach. Tennis courts, restaurants and bars round off the fun.

In Funchal's hotel district on the promenade there are two pools that charge for admission (*Lido* and *Ponta Gorda, 3.10 euros each*). In addition to steps leading down to the sea, they have proper swimming pools, paddling pools for children,

spaces for sunbathing and sanitary facilities. The sea pool *Poças do Gomes*, situated between Praia Formosa and the western end of the promenade by the Doca do Cavacas restaurant, is somewhat smaller, cheaper *(1.60 euros)* and has no man-made pool. In the historic quarter opposite the Igreja do Socorro, the *Barreirinha* pool charges *1.60 euros* while a little pebbly beach next to the São Tiago fort costs nothing and is popular with the children who live close by.

TENNIS
One of the nicest tennis courts can be found in the park of Quinta Magnolia. *Rua Dr Pita | tel. 2 91 76 45 98*

ENTERTAINMENT

There is always something going on at the weekend in Funchal – usually musical events, and often live music. Big concerts are sometimes held in the *Madeira Tecnopolo (Caminho da Penteada)*, and **INSIDER TIP** smaller events regularly take place on the premises of the *FNAC* book/electronics store *(Madeira Shopping | Caminho Santa Quitéria | www.fnac.pt).* On weekdays, too, Madeirans like to go out. There are good bars and clubs in, for example, *Rua da Imperatriz Dona Amélia*, *Rua da Carreira* and on the *Promenade in the Lido district.* Normally not much happens there before midnight, and in the dance clubs things don't really get going until 2am. Folklore shows in hotels and restaurants, by contrast, generally start after dinner. Admission is charged for the clubs, but a drink is often included in the price.

CAFÉ DO TEATRO
By day tourists and locals drink their coffee In the theatre café; in the evening the trendy crowd take over. There is a mixed, tolerant clientele: alternative-minded students, chic yuppies, and sometimes holidaymakers who didn't come to Madeira to sleep, dance the night away to DJ sounds or live music. *Sun–Thu 8am–1am, Fri/Sat 10am–4am | next to Teatro Municipal | Av. Arriaga | www.cafe doteatro.com*

Open to interpretation: a casino in the shape of a crown of thorns

CASINO DA MADEIRA

Diners and clubbers, gamblers and architecture aficionados: all of these rave about the casino, an extravagant construction designed by the Brazilian cult architect Oscar Niemeyer in the shape of a crown of thorns that resembles the cathedral of Brasília. Night owls come to try their luck at the gaming tables and dance to live music in the Copacabana disco. *Av. do Infante | www.casinodamadeira.com*

INSIDER TIP ▶ CHEGA DE SAUDADE

The name says it all: enough yearning – it's party time now! That's the motto of this innovative mix of restaurant, café, trendy bar and dance club. Not only that: items from the designer furnishings are often on sale. At weekends jazz or alternative music are regularly on the bill. *Mon–Thu 9am–midnight, Fri 9am–2am, Sat 6pm–2am | Rua dos Aranhas 20 | chega desaudadecafe.blogspot.com*

JAM JAZZ CLUB / VESPAS

Two locations under one roof: uphill from the cruise liner harbour, both lovers of live jazz and clubbers find what they are looking for. *Thu–Sun 11pm–4am | Av. Sá Carneiro 60*

KATZ – CAFÉ & NIGHT CLUB

A new hip place with dance floor, café and bar lounge on the ocean promenade. At the weekends the action consists of concerts, DJs and themed parties. *Fri–Sat 11pm–4am | Jardins Panorâmicos | Passeio Público Marítimo*

MARCELINO, PÃO E VINHO

Every evening from 10pm a variety of performers play fado in a rustic bar ambience. The musicians and the singing owner Senhor Amaro only take a break on Sundays. Guests are expected to consume drinks and food for at least 7.50 euros. *Travessa das Torres 22 | old quarter*

TEATRO MUNICIPAL BALTAZAR DIAS

The municipal theatre is often used as a concert hall. Madeira's classical orchestra *(www.ocmadeira.com)* performs in the Neoclassical auditorium, and the mandolin orchestra *(www.madeira mandolinorchestra.com)*, which plays in the ● English Church *(Rua do Quebra Costas 18)* every Friday during the season, also entertains visitors here on some evenings. *Av. Arriaga | tel. 2 91 23 35 69*

WHERE TO STAY

CHOUPANA HILLS RESORT ☺

Wood, stone, basketwork – the typical materials of Madeira, applied in an exotic and contemporary style to furnish luxurious bungalows built on stilts high above Funchal. Thanks to environmentally sound production of the timber for building, water from the hotel's own spring and its sewage treatment system, the Choupana is certified as an eco hotel. The ● extensive spa is one of the best in Europe. Good restaurant. *64 rooms | Travessa do Largo da Choupana | tel 2 91 20 60 20 | www.choupanahills.com | Expensive*

GOLDEN RESIDENCE

New four-star apartment hotel with modern design and health facilities. Preventive health programmes and a big spa. *172 rooms | Rua do Cabrestante 25 | near the Forum Madeira shopping centre | tel. 2 91 71 01 00 | www.goldenresidencehotel.com | Moderate–Expensive*

HOTEL APARTAMENTO DA SÉ

You can hardly be more central at a reasonable price: the basic but pleasant apartments with well-equipped kitchens

The terrace of Reid's Palace in the morning hours – it fills up in the afternoons

are just a few yards from the cathedral. On the roof terrace guests enjoy the use of loungers and a ☼ bar with a sea view. *40 rooms | Rua do Sabão 56 | tel. 2 912 146 00 | www.aparthotelse-madeira. com | Budget*

PORTO SANTA MARIA

This elegant and modern house is situated between the old fishermen's quarter and the seafront promenade. Warm colours, sunny terrace, a small indoor and outdoor pool. *146 rooms | Av. do Mar 50 | tel. 2 912 06 700 | www.portostamaria. com | Expensive*

QUINTA DA CASA BRANCA

A low-slung glass construction in the middle of a well-tended quinta garden with a historic main building. Every room in this award-winning boutique hotel has a private patio. *43 rooms | Rua da Casa Branca 7 | tel. 2 917 00 770 | www.quinta casabranca.pt | Expensive*

QUINTA MÃE DOS HOMENS ☼

Charming and elegant historic house with a pretty garden and pool – and a view across Funchal. The 22 studios and apartments are ideal for self-caterers. *Rua Mãe dos Homens 39 | tel. 2 912 04 410 | www.qmdh.com | Moderate*

REID'S PALACE ⭐ ●

The legend lives on – and, while keeping all its traditional grandeur, has given itself a contemporary facelift. By coming here for the stylish English afternoon tea (28 euros, no casual dress) on the terrace with a view of Funchal harbour or to the French gourmet restaurant *Les Faunes*, non-residents too can experience some of the distinctive charm of this luxury hotel, which has been in business since 1891. Under new management the emphasis is on families (supervised children's pool) and health and beauty: the old laundry has been converted to a spa bathed in light. A subtropical park leads down in steps from the hotel to the sea. *163 rooms | Estrada Monumental 139 | tel. 2 91 71 71 71 | www.reidspalace.com | Expensive*

RESIDENCIAL DA MARIAZINHA
Typical Madeiran atmosphere in a restored house in the old Santa Maria quarter of the city. The courtyard is small, and the rooms are spacious. *10 rooms | Rua de Santa Maria 155 | tel. 2 91 22 02 39 | www.residencialmariazinha.com | Moderate*

RESIDENCIAL QUEIMADA DE BAIXO
This basic guesthouse in a traffic-calmed street between the cathedral and the city hall square is a good base for exploring the city centre, as everything is within a few minutes' walk. *10 rooms | Rua da Queimada de Baixo 46 | tel. 2 91 21 32 50 | Budget*

VILA VICÊNCIA
Three privately run villas in a garden above the hotel district not far from the seafront promenade. Furnishings in typical Madeiran style. *29 rooms | Rua da Casa Branca 45 | tel. 2 91 77 15 27 | www.vilavicencia.com | Budget–Moderate*

INFORMATION

DIRECÇÃO REGIONAL DO TURISMO
Av. Arriaga 18 | tel. 2 91 21 19 00 | www.madeiraturismo.com
Another tourist office: *Centro Comercial Monumental Lido | Estrada Monumental 284 | tel. 2 91 77 52 54*

WHERE TO GO

CABO GIRÃO AND FAJÃ DOS PADRES
● (129 D–E 5) (*𝄢 H 8*)
The so-called ⛷ Cape of Return, 8 mi west of Funchal and close to Câmara de Lobos, has some of the world's highest cliffs. The drop to the water measures 580 m and is almost vertical. From the viewing terrace those who dare to look down can see that the narrow strip of land at the base of the cliffs is used for growing wine and vegetables. Very close to Cabo Girão a ⛷ cable lift *(5 euros)* originally built as a means of transport for the farmers connects the village of *Rancho* to the fields bordering the coast. For an even more spectacular experience, go another 2 km (1.2 mi) and take the glass lift *(Wed–Mon 11am–7pm | 7.50 euros)* down to ● Fajã dos Padres, a private beach *(tel. 2 91 94 45 38 | www.fajadospadres.com)* with a lunch-time restaurant (*Budget*) and holiday homes (*Moderate*) beneath palm trees, a jetty, vines and a plantation for tropical fruit. The estate was originally founded by Jesuits, and the remains of a chapel can be seen.

CÂMARA DE LOBOS
(129 F5 –6) (*𝄢 J 8*)
Lobos marinhos, monk seals that lived in the bay at the time of the discovery of Madeira, gave this fishing port between two rocky cliffs 9 km (5.6 mi) west of Funchal its name. With 17,000 inhabitants it is the second-largest town on the island. João Gonçalves Zarco founded the settlement and built a little church by the harbour. In the early 18th century the *Capela Nossa Senhora da Conceição* was taken over by a charitable brotherhood of fishermen and remodelled. Today the interior is decorated with paintings depicting scenes of catching fish.

To this day the fishery and a modest amount of boat building dominate daily life in Câmara de Lobos, but neither of these activities is particularly lucrative, and many local families live in poverty. Away from the picturesque harbour views the town has a raft of social problems. Winston Churchill set up his easel on a little terrace to paint the harbour scene with its gaily coloured fishing boats when he stayed on Madeira at the turn of 1949–50. A plaque at that ☀ *miradouro* on the main street commemorates the great statesman's artistic streak.

Walk through the fishermen's quarter with its pubs and bars, which also attract a young crowd from Funchal, to reach the upper part of town, site of the parish church of *São Sebastião*, adorned with blue and yellow Baroque tiles. On the *Largo da República* behind it the buildings have been renewed, with two white cubes for a restaurant and a café; only the historic pavilion in the centre

of the island's best wine-growing areas: *Estreito de Câmara de Lobos*. Every year at the time of the grape harvest, a big festival held here keeps ancient Madeiran traditions alive: from the procession of the wine farmers, who bring their grapes to be pressed, to the treading of the grapes. For a stylish little place to stay, look no further than the modern complex of the *Quinta do Estreito (46 rooms | Rua José da Costa | tel. 2 91 91 05 30 | www.quinta doestreitomadeira.com | Moderate–Expensive)*, which was built around a historic residence, and offers its guests a pool, garden, gourmet restaurant and a little rustic tavern.

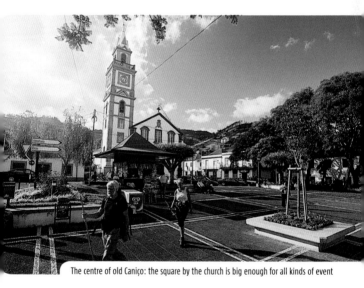

The centre of old Caniço: the square by the church is big enough for all kinds of event

was spared. The place for swimming lies below the square. Above the market hall, diners at the bright modern *Vila do Peixe* restaurant *(Rua Dr João Freitas 30 | tel. 2 91 09 99 09 | Moderate–Expensive)* can make their own selection of fresh fish and have it grilled.

Higher up from Câmara de Lobos is one

CANIÇO (131 E–F 6) (*ω N 8*)

Fields of onions were the hallmark of the region around Caniço (pop. 15 ,000), 11 km (6.8 mi) east of Funchal, before tourism arrived here in the 1970s. Foreigners, especially Germans, built houses on the land that slopes down to the coast, and some massive rows of apartment blocks and large hotels were also constructed. Along with neighbouring *Garajau*, the new district of *Caniço de Baixo* has now become Madeira's second-biggest centre of tourism after Funchal. However, on the second weekend in May, the 'onion festival' is still celebrated to keep the memory of old times alive.

The original settlement of Caniço clusters around the 18th-century *parish church*. Its interior is now fairly plain, as the Baroque altars were painted white and sparingly adorned with gold leaf.

Not far away, the ● *Quinta Splendida* hotel *(166 rooms | Estrada da Ponta da Oliveira 11 | tel. 2 91 93 04 00 | www.quintasplendida.com | Expensive)* lies in the middle of a luxuriant botanical garden. It has a spacious new spa, 25 designer suites to match, a pool and a charming gourmet restaurant in the historic quinta house. The hotel garden is also open to non-residents, and guided tours are also on offer (ask at the reception for times). As many of the trees, flowers and herbs that grow here are marked by name, the estate is officially regarded as a botanical garden.

Inn & Art, which originated as a private house with a gallery, is a complex of villas, apartments and restaurant *(27 rooms | Rua Robert Baden Powell 61–62 | tel. 2 91 93 82 00 | www.innart.com | Moderate).*

Excellent fish and meat dishes from the grill are served up at *Le Buffet (Caniço de Baixo | Rua D Francisco Santana 1 | tel. 2 91 93 65 49 | www.madeira-lebuffet.com | Moderate).*

CURRAL DAS FREIRAS
(129 F 2) *(𝄞 J 5–6)*

'The nuns' byre' is the literal meaning of the name of the island's deepest valley. It refers to the former owners of the land, the Sisters of St Clare from the Santa Clara convent in Funchal, who used the bowl-like valley as a pasture for their animals. In the 16th and 17th centuries, a time when the island was repeatedly attacked by pirates, the nuns retreated to the protection offered by the 700-metre-high mountain walls several times. In 1566, after surviving unharmed an especially brutal raid by privateers, they gave thanks by building a chapel. Visit the ✴ INSIDER TIP cemetery of the church that was later built on the same site to enjoy a wonderful view of the lower valley and the higher ground up to the viewing point of *Eira do Serrado.*

Sweet chestnuts are the speciality of the village (pop. 1700), which lies 20 km (12.4 mi) north of Funchal and is visited by lots of day-trippers. The inhabitants make liqueur, cake, bread and soup from the chestnuts. For those who plan to stay here overnight, the comfortable ✴ *Estalagem Eira do Serrado (25 rooms | tel. 2 91 71 00 60 | www.eiradoserrado.com | Budget)* with its sauna, indoor pool and restaurant is recommended.

JARDIM BOTÂNICO ● (130 C 5) *(𝄞 L 7)*

More than 2500 beautiful tropical and subtropical plants thrive on the grounds of the *Quinta do Bom Sucesso* ('great success'), an area of approx. 4 ha which once belonged to the Reid family of hotel owners and is situated about 300 m higher than the centre of Funchal. Hidden away in the lush greenery and surrounded by trees, some of which are over 100 years old, a *café terrace offers refreshments.* At the northern edge of the park is the lower terminus of the cable car, which takes passengers across the impressive Ribeira de João Gomes valley to the Largo das Babosas in Monte *(8.25 euros, return ticket 12.75 euros).* At the western tip of the Jardim Botânico a ✴ *miradouro* commands a fantastic view of Funchal and the bay.

The villa houses the *Museu de História Natural*, a charmingly old-fashioned natural history museum. Admission to the garden includes the price for a visit to the tropical birds in the adjacent *Jardim dos Loiros (Jardim Botânico | Caminho do Meio | daily 9am–6pm | admission 3 euros | www.madeirabotanicalgarden.com)*. From here it is a short walk downhill to the privately owned *Jardim Quinta da Boa Vista*, where there are fine old trees, a little INSIDER TIP terrace where tea and cake are served, and an outstanding display of orchids *(Rua do Lombo da Boa Vista | Mon–Sat 9am–6pm | admission 4.50 euros)*.

MONTE (130 C 4) (*M L 4*)

As early as the 18th century Monte's cool climate, lush vegetation, beautiful views of the sea and closeness to the capital of the island (8 km, 4.9 mi) made it a sought-after address for wealthy and elegant Europeans. Even the last em-

peror of Austria, Karl I, resided here in 1921, when the Machado family offered him their *Quinta do Monte* as a place of refuge in his exile. This estate, long in a state of decay, has now been returned to its former splendour, and the restored garden and tea terrace welcome visitors for a stroll and refreshments. The café is housed in the imposing Malakoff Tower, which was built in the 18th century by the owner of the day, James Gordon. From here the views of Monte and Funchal are simply wonderful *(Quinta Jardins do Imperador | Caminho do Pico | Mon–Sat 9.30am–5.30pm | admission 6 euros)*.

Karl I was buried in the *pilgrimage church of Nossa Senhora do Monte*, which stands on a hill above the main square, Largo da Fonte. From here the lovely *municipal garden (free admission)* extends down the valley. According to a legend, in the 16th century the Virgin Mary appeared to a shepherd girl here. At the place of this vision, the girl's father later

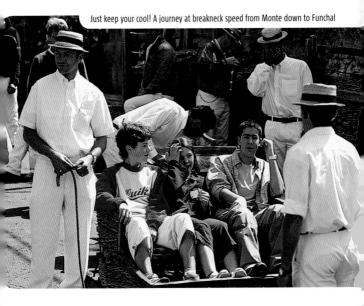

Just keep your cool! A journey at breakneck speed from Monte down to Funchal

found a statue of the Virgin, in honour of which the villagers built a chapel. In front of the steps that lead up to the church, the men who steer the ★ ● *basket sleds* wait for customers, whom they then propel about 2km (1.2 mi) downhill in antique sleds *(carros de cestos) (Mon–Sat 9am–6pm, Sun 9am–1pm | 12.50 euros/ person)*. This ride down the road on runners, without any snow and amid motorised traffic, is unique in the world, which makes it one of the tourist highlights of a stay on Madeira.

The sledmen form a kind of guild with hereditary membership – for men only. They wear their distinctive costume consisting of white trousers and shirt, a blue jacket and a straw hat. They steer and brake the sleds with their shoes, which are reinforced with a special kind of rubber. Their cooperative now organises the return transport of the sleds on trucks. In bygone days the sledmen had to laboriously pull or carry their vehicles back up the hill. The journey no longer goes right down into the centre of Funchal, as it once did, but only as far as Livramento, where expensive taxis lie in wait but where there is also a bus connection into town.

Back in 1894 a cog railway went into operation to provide a fast connection between Monte and Funchal. It closed down in 1943, and now modern cable cars make the journey.

The cable car terminus is close to the INSIDER TIP **tropical palace garden** in Monte. In the 18th century the Quinta do Prazer occupied this site, and in the late 19th century built a palatial villa and laid out extensive gardens. This villa became the *Monte Palace Hotel.* After the Second World War the condition of the grounds became more and more ruinous, until in the 1980s José Berardo ('Joe Gold'), who had made a fortune in South Africa, took over the decayed estate of the Monte Palace Hotel and turned it into the enchanting *Jardim Tropical Monte Palace, a tropical garden and a place for art.* In addition to a host of laurel trees, palms and ferns, the garden is filled with azulejo pictures and other works of art, and has ponds with koi carp, Buddha statues and oriental gateways. And if that's not enough, visitors can admire the largest vase ever to have been made on a potter's wheel – it stands on the banks of the swan pond *(daily 9.30am–6pm | admission 10 euros | Caminho das Babosas 4 | www.montepalace.com)*.

BASKET SLEDS

A British merchant from Monte is said to have invented this means of transport, which is unique to Madeira. He was looking for a way of travelling quickly and comfortably to his office in Funchal. In those days there were no roads on the island, but only steep, narrow paved paths, which were often unsuitable for a horse and carriage, a donkey or a mule. Goods were therefore largely transported on foot. The old, the sick and the wealthy were carried in hammocks or sedan chairs. In Funchal the use of ox sleds began in the mid-19th century. At the same time the lighter basket sled *(carro de cesto)* was invented. Two strong men were all that was required to push it off, steer its downhill course, and above all to pull it back up to where the descent started.

High above Funchal: the Oriental Garden, part of the Jardim Tropical Monte Palace

A little way uphill from Monte, the terrace of the *Quinta Terreiro da Luta* restaurant *(Sítio Terreiro da Luta | tel. 291784346 | Moderate)* is a pleasant spot to take a drink at the bar or relax with a cup of coffee in the old garden.

PALHEIRO GARDENS ★
(131 D–E 5) *(爪 M 7)*

On the road to Camacha, 9 km (5.6 mi) east of Funchal at 600 m above sea level, one of the island's most beautiful and varied gardens can be found: the Palheiro Gardens. The *Quinta do Palheiro Ferreiro* once belonged to the Count of Carvalhal. In the 18th century he used the grand house there as a hunting lodge, but his descendants wasted the family fortune, and so in 1885 the estate became the country seat of the Blandy family, a British dynasty of wine merchants. They built themselves a new residence on the grounds. This private country villa is surrounded by a carefully planned English garden with superb subtropical plants. Behind the chapel the garden opens out to luxuriant stands of strelitzias and a water-lily pond; in front of the quinta the *sunken garden* unfolds a gorgeous world of colours. The Palheiro Gardens are also famous for their camellias and a variety of proteas, which Mildred Blandy imported to the island from South Africa *(Mon–Fri 9am–4.30pm | admission 10.50 euros)*.

The shady *teahouse* is the place to rest after walking round the garden. It is situated between the golf course and the *Casa Velha do Palheiro (37 rooms | Rua de Estalagem 23 | São Gonçalo | tel. 291790350 | www.casa-velha.com | Expensive)*. This luxury hotel stands within the historic walls of the former residence of the Count of Carvalhal. It has been extended through the construction of a spa and a restaurant that serves exquisite food *(Expensive)*.

THE SOUTH

Fishing villages by the sea, narrow terraces for growing bananas, a bare high-altitude plateau, vineyards and charming little bays – no more than a few miles from the island's lively capital, the landscape of Madeira reveals its unspoilt natural beauty.

From steep coastal rocks, waterfalls cascade onto little beaches and winding roads, dense growths of agapanthus line the wayside, houses are surrounded with colourful blooms, and shady picnic spots with stone-built grills for cooking *espetada* tempt travellers to take a break. Tourism may be on the up in the south of Madeira, but there are still plenty of opportunities to discover the region without joining the crowd.

On walking trails through the villages that lie above the coast you can gain a remarkable impression of how country people live here. Old women in headscarves labour on tiny potato fields, or men climb across the terraces carrying 80 kg of bananas over their shoulders.

This is all in great contrast to the scene in the coastal towns: the old trading port of Ribeira Grande, the Mediterranean-like community of Ponta do Sol, and Calheta, a former centre of the sugar-cane industry which now benefits from the bright sand of its beach, provide pleasant living conditions for their residents. In coastal villages such as Madalena, Jardim and Paúl do Mar, growing numbers of keen surfers who have come from far and wide rub shoulders with fishermen and banana farmers.

Photo: Bay near Ribeira Brava

From the coast to the plateau – the south of Madeira can be pretty and lively, or rugged and sleepy

CALHETA

(126–127 C–D 1–2) (*C–D 5–6*)

The main town in the southwest (pop. 3100) stretches from the coast to the heights along a narrow river valley dominated by a road.

A few chimneys of stone or brick and historic distillery equipment on the palm-fringed seafront promenade testify to the importance that sugar cane once had for the local economy.

Today Calheta puts its faith in tourism: a large marina has been created, light-coloured sand dumped to make beaches and a spectacular arts centre built on the cliffs. Every year after harvest time (round about April) a sugar-cane festival is celebrated, and in the park at the western end of the bay of Vila Calheta – as the town is officially called – the congregation of the church builds a wonderful **INSIDER TIP** nativity scene each Christmas – with life-size figures and often featuring real animals.

CALHETA

CASA DAS MUDAS – CENTRO DAS ARTES ●

The bold architecture of the arts centre is home to exhibitions, and sometimes, INSIDER TIP international cinema is shown here too. The restaurant with its 🔆 panorama terrace (tel. 2 91 82 73 16 | Moderate) serves up a contemporary the island that has remained intact. In spring the historic equipment is regularly used to distil the clear, fiery sugar-cane spirit known as *aguardente* and to produce *mel de cana*, sugar-cane syrup. There is a room for tastings (1 euro) and a shop. *Open for visits Mon–Fri 8am–6pm, Sat/Sun 9am–1pm and 2–6pm | free admission | Av. D. Manuel I. 29 | www.engenhosdacalheta.com*

Classy, cosy, tasteful: the library and bar in the Hotel Atrio

take on local and Portuguese dishes. *Tue–Sun 10am–1pm and 2–6pm | admission 5 euros | Vale dos Amores | tel. 2 91 82 09 00 | www.centrodasartes.com*

IGREJA DO ESPÍRITO SANTO

The parish church was begun in the 15th century and altered a number of times. The decorative work around the door is a survivor from the early period, and it's also worth going inside to see the carved Mudéjar-style ceiling and the tabernacle made of ebony and silver in the side aisle.

SOCIEDADE DOS ENGENHOS DA CALHETA

What lies behind this unwieldy name is one of the few sugar-cane mills on

In the marina there are several modern restaurants with spacious terraces, most of which serve Madeiran food.

ROCHA MAR

An upmarket marisqueira, popular for its fish and seafood dishes. *Av. D. Manuel I. (opposite the marina) | tel. 2 91 82 36 00 | Moderate*

SWIMMING

There is golden yellow sand on Madeira's sunny coast! The two man-made beaches at Calheta attract a few tourists from

THE SOUTH

the Calheta Beach Hotel, but most of all Madeiran weekenders – and the beach that was created using Moroccan sand is seldom crowded. Palm trees on the promenade, pleasant bars and restaurants and a quiet marina lend the place an air of Caribbean holiday.

PARAGLIDING

In *Arco da Calheta* the *International Paragliding Center* organises passenger flights by paraglider. Amateur pilots can also use the landing strip, and in addition it is possible to book **INSIDER TIP** flights in a small private aircraft. *Rua Achada de Santo Antão 199 | mobile tel. 9 64 13 39 07 | www.madeira-paragliding.com*

WHALE-WATCHING ☺

'Ribeira Brava' is the name of a restored fishing boat that leaves the harbour of Calheta on a regular basis for whale-watching trips. The operators take care to approach the whales gently and not to disturb them. The team at *Lobosonda* is committed to the protection of whales and supports scientific research by providing statistics on its sightings of whales and dolphins to the whaling museum in Caniçal. *Mobile tel. 9 68 40 09 80 | www.lobosonda.com*

WHERE TO STAY

ATRIO ⭐
A complex built in the style of a quinta, with individually designed rooms, a heated outdoor pool, hanging gardens and a bar with fireplace. This is an excellent base for a walking holiday, as there is a library with hiking guidebooks, and the reception lends flashlights free of charge for walking through tunnels. The hotel team includes two mountain guides who are available for tours. For breakfast there are many homemade

treats and herbs from the hotel garden. *14 rooms | Lombo dos Moinhos Acima Estreito da Calheta | tel. 2 91 82 04 00 | www.atrio-madeira.com | Moderate*

CASA DO CALHAU GRANDE
Six renovated historic stone houses which can be rented separately. Each has self-catering accommodation for two to four persons in grounds with a pool on a mountainside above Calheta. *Caminho do Massapez 10 | Arco de Calheta | mobile tel. 9 62 80 66 26 | www.casadocalhaugrande.com | Moderate*

WHERE TO GO

JARDIM DO MAR AND PAÚL DO MAR
These two fishing villages are among the oldest settlements on the island. *Jardim do Mar (126 C 1) (⌀ B 5)*, 5 km (3.1 mi) from Calheta, with its population of 250, is surrounded by the fertile land of a coastal plateau. From the main square in the historic centre a lane leads down

MARCO POLO HIGHLIGHTS

⭐ **Atrio**
Stylish accommodation with the atmosphere of a modern country house in Calheta → p. 53

⭐ **Paúl da Serra**
A high-altitude plateau that feels like Scotland – with breathtaking views → p. 55

⭐ **Achadas da Cruz**
The cable lift descends almost vertically to the fields by the coast → p. 56

⭐ **Boca da Encumeada**
In good weather a view of both coasts at once → p. 59

Banana plants and holiday homes: Madalena do Mar

to the sea, where a fort once stood and a modern promenade has now been built. It is reached by passing through the crooked alleyways in the centre of the village. A small stone-built house with high terraces right on the *esplanada* houses the *Portinho* restaurant *(Sítio da Pie-dade | tel. 2 918 27135 | Budget)*, which specialises in seafood. The hotel *Jardim do Mar (30 rooms | Sítio da Piedade | tel. 2 918 22 00 | www.hoteljardimdomar. com | Moderate)* is furnished in the style of a country house.

Paúl do Mar (120 B 6) *(𝄢 B 4)* with its old centre nestles right by the sea. A large rubber tree shades the main square of the village, which has just under 1000 residents. Walk downhill and left to reach the enlarged and re-developed harbour with its statue of a fisherman. The place to swim is at the foot of the statue and on the slipway for the colourful fishing boats. The cliffs rear up almost vertically behind the harbour

to a height of almost 300 m. For deli-cious fish dishes with a sea view try the *Bay Side Cafe (6am–11pm | Paúl do Mar | near the harbour | tel. 2 918 72 0 22 | Budget–Moderate);* accommodation is available in the *Aparthotel Paúl do Mar* at the western end of the bay; it has a pool *(60 studios | Ribeira das Galinhas | tel. 2 918 70 00 50 | www.hotelpauldomar. com | Moderate)*.

MADALENA DO MAR
(127 E 3) *(𝄢 D–E 6)*

Many wealthy residents of Funchal own weekend homes in this high-class coastal village (pop. 700). It is strung out on a long bay at the foot of steep terraced slopes used for growing bananas, some 3.5 km (2.1 mi) from Calheta. The *Restau-rante Praia Mar* on the new promenade *(Banda d'Além | tel. 2 919 74164 | preia-mar.wordpress.com | Moderate)* with an attractive wooden terrace facing the sea and fish specialities is a popular spot.

PAÚL DA SERRA ⭐
(122 A–C 6) (𝄞 E–F 4)

This plateau, 11 km (6.8 mi) northeast of Calheta, is reminiscent of a moor landscape in the uplands of Britain. Only sturdy plants like grasses, gorse and bracken can cope with the inhospitable climate at an altitude of over 1000 m. The ground here stores rainwater like a sponge and is the source of levadas which distribute water to many parts of the island and channel it to hydroelectric plants. Dozens of wind generators also turn their blades here high in the sky. Strong winds often blow up on the plateau, and when, as so often, the winds are joined by fog, then it is easy to understand why plans to construct an airport up here were quickly shelved. In good weather however there are stunning views from the ☀ panoramic road.

About halfway across the plain, a road descends to the valley of *Rabaçal*, where walks lead to the *Risco waterfall* and to a valley basin in the rocks named *25 Fontes* (25 springs). The place to stay on the plateau is the modern *Estalagem Pico da Urze* (27 rooms | Sítio do Ovil | tel. 2 91 82 01 50 | www.hotelpicodaurze.com | Budget–Moderate, frequent special offers).

PRAZERES (120 C 6) (𝄞 B–C 4–5)

This village (pop. 700, 7.5 km (4.7 mi) northwest of Calheta) is an excellent base for walking in the west of the island: on trails going down to Paúl do Mar, along a number of little levadas or up to the Paúl da Serra plateau. The only attractions in the village itself are the *Quinta Pedagógica*, a botanical park with animals and a shady **INSIDER TIP** café (daily 9am–8pm, in summer until 9pm | www.prazeresdaquinta.com | admission: garden free, zoo 1 euro) and the parish church with its two towers. It dates from the 18th century but was restored in 1940. For dining in cosy surroundings try the *Restaurante Chico* (Sítio da Igreja | tel. 2 91 82 28 36 | Budget–Moderate), for an overnight stay the ☀ environmentally friendly hotel *Jardim Atlântico* (97 rooms | Lombo da Rocha | tel. 2 91 82 02 20 | www.jardimatlantico.com | Expensive) with its sports and spa facilities.

PONTA DO PARGO

(120 A–B 3–4) (𝄞 A 2–3) The main sight in this community of six scattered districts (pop. 1300) is the lighthouse (farol) in Salão de Baixo, which went into operation in 1922 on the Rocha da Vigia.

In the lower part of Madeira's best-looking lighthouse a permanent exhibition shows photos of the lighthouses on the island (Mon–Fri 10am–midday and 2pm–

The moon shines on the lighthouse of Ponta do Pargo

5pm | free admission). From the foot of the lighthouse there is a wonderful view of the sheer coast, which drops 312 m (341 yd) into the sea here. In 2012 the third and largest golf course on Madeira is opening on this site. Nick Faldo designed the 18-hole course, which takes players across the plateau around the lighthouse. The modest village centre of Ponta do Pargo (Salão de Cima) lies around the church of *São Pedro,* which *possesses an attractive painted ceiling, the work of a local Belgian artist.*

FOOD & DRINK

A CARRETA

Hearty *espetadas* and other specialities typical of the island are on the menu in this simple rural guesthouse, which is also popular among hikers as a place to stay the night (*Budget*). *Lombada Velha | tel. 2 91 88 21 63 | Moderate*

O FORNO

Marta Silva from Fajã da Ovelha welcomes guests to her new restaurant: with reasonably priced daily specials and her classic dishes such as rabbit and squid. *Salão (on the main road next to the cemetery) | mobile tel. 9 66 07 28 79 | Moderate*

WHERE TO STAY

QUINTA DO ESPIGÃO ☼

A charmingly furnished private house in a lonely spot on a wooded cliff. *3 rooms | Caminho de Portela Abaixo 1 | Serrado | mobile tel. 9 65 88 23 17 | www.convista. net | Moderate–Expensive*

WHERE TO GO

ACHADAS DA CRUZ ★
(120 C 2) (*Ⓜ B 1–2*)

A modern cable car *(teleférico)* is the principal attraction of this little village (pop. 200) 10 km (6.2 mi) northeast of Ponta do Pargo, which has a sleepy air. The cabins of the cable lift sway downward, seemingly vertically, to cover the 300 metres difference in height to the fields by the rocky coast below. *Return trip 3 euros*

CAPELA DA NOSSA SENHORA DA BOA MORTE/CABO (120 B 2–3) (*Ⓜ B 2*)

This little pilgrimage church was built in the early 20th century on a lonely promontory, some distance away from the nearest hamlet, Cabo (pop. approx. 50), 4 km (2.5 mi) northeast of Ponta do Pargo. A hidden spring that bubbles up beneath its walls was used by farmers' wives as a source of water. They are said to have seen the Virgin Mary a number of times. In late July or early August a INSIDER TIP procession is held in honour of the Virgin – one of the few occasions when the chapel is opened.

FAJÃ DA OVELHA ⚘
(120 B 5) (*∅ B 4*)

12 km (7.5 mi) south of Ponta do Pargo, this settlement (pop. 1100) is perched on a raise high above the Atlantic. The church of *São João Batista* with its lovely bell tower dates from the 17th century. A few typical old houses remain in the village itself. Fajã da Ovelha commands a fine view of the cliffs, with Paúl do Mar at the bottom – best seen from the terrace of the *Restaurante Precipício (Sítio de São Lourenço | tel. 2 91 87 24 25 | Budget)*, which serves down-to-earth fare and fresh fish. For the INSIDER TIP best *poncha* in this area go to the snack bar *Moinho (tel. 2 91 87 21 81)* in the district of Maloeira. It is packed and has bags of atmosphere, especially at weekends.

RIBEIRA BRAVA

(128 C 4–5) (*∅ G 7*) This coastal town with its 6000 inhabitants is located at the mouth of a wide river (ribeira) that turns into a 'wild' (brava) torrent after rain.

Thanks to the fast highway to Funchal it is popular with Madeirans as a place to stay during the summer heat or at weekends. This means that the expansion of the town for more and more new apartment blocks is rapidly devouring the surrounding banana fields. Numerous cafés in the shade on the main square, which is open to the sea on one side, tempt visitors to stop here for a while.

The 'wild river' can live up to its name, as the people of Ribeira Grande discovered to their cost in February 2010: after heavy rainfall it destroyed houses and slopes in Serra de Água, which lies

What would you give for a deckchair? – the pebble beach at Ribeira Brava

at a higher elevation than the town centre, as well as bridges, parts of the coast road and the beach promenade in Ribeira Grande. Following work to clear up the damage, the locals and their guests can once again enjoy the long stony beach.

SIGHTSEEING

OLD QUARTER

The historic core of the town can be found on either side of the pedestrianised *Rua do Visconde*. Here, little shops supply everyday needs, and some of them have even incorporated a bar to serve drinks. The *Câmara Municipal* (town hall), a pink-painted quinta dating from the late 18th century, lies hidden behind the tall old trees of an attractive park.

IGREJA DE SÃO BENTO

The most conspicuous feature of the parish church is its steeple with a blue-and-white pattern in tiles and a globe (an armillary sphere), the symbol of the Portuguese explorers. The foundation stone of the church was laid as early as 1440, which makes it one of the oldest places of worship on the island. During the Baroque period, however, it was given a completely new look. The original furnishings include a baptismal font donated by King Manuel I of Portugal in the chapel to the right of the entrance and the Manueline pulpit.

MUSEU ETNOGRÁFICO DA MADEIRA

Madeira's folk museum is housed in a fine 17th-century residence that once belonged to the Order of St Clare. The exhibitions in these stylish surroundings document traditional crafts, means of transport and methods of cultivating and harvesting crops on the island. In the little souvenir shop you can buy woven fabrics that were made in the museum. Part of the museum is used as a gallery to display changing exhibitions of contemporary art. *Mon closed | admission 2.50 euros | Rua São Francisco 24*

FOOD & DRINK

BORDA D'AGUA ●

A bright modern building on the esplanade with a seaside terrace and specialities such as *fejoada marisco* (seafood stew) and scabbard fish in wine and garlic. *Rua Engenheiro Pereira Ribeiro | tel. 2 91 95 76 97 | Moderate*

WHERE TO STAY

HOTEL BRAVAMAR

Centrally located and good value for money. *70 rooms | Rua Gago Coutinho e Sacadura Cabral 2a | tel. 2 91 95 22 20 | www.hotel-bravamar.com | Budget*

HOTEL DO CAMPO ☺

On the slopes some way above the town, this hotel, certified for its green policies, combines luxury with a quiet and restful stay – and boasts a magnificent view as well. *34 rooms | Estrada da Banda de Além 25 | Ribeira Brava | tel. 2 91 95 02 70 | www.hoteldocampo.com | Expensive*

INSIDER TIP ▶ QUINTA DO CABOUCO ☺

High up in the hills, a historic country house with an organic garden from which guests can help themselves. *3 rooms | Caminho do Cabouco | mobile tel 9 18 69 69 96 | www.quintadocabouco.com | Budget*

INFORMATION

TOURIST INFORMATION

Forte de São Bento | tel. 2 91 95 16 75

WHERE TO GO

BOCA DA ENCUMEADA ★ ⚜
(129 D 1) (𝄞 H 4)

13 km (8.1 mi) north of Ribeira Brava and some 1000 m above sea level, this 'mouth' *(boca)* in the mountain range opens up to provide a thrilling panorama: of the north coast with São Vicente, the plateau of Paúl da Serra, the valley of Serra de Água and the wild heart of the mountains with their ravines and peaks. A number of demanding walks start from the pass – over Pico do Jorge and Pico das Torrinhas to Pico Ruivo, for example. The accommodation options here are: a little below the Boca da Encumeada, the cosy and elegant ⚜ *Pousada dos Vinháticos* with its log cabin annexe *(21 rooms | Serra de Água | tel. 2 91 95 23 44 | www. pousadadosvinhaticos.com | Budget)* or the ⚜ *Residencial Encumeada (49 rooms | Feiteirais | Serra de Água | tel. 2 91 95 12 82 | www.residencialencumeada. com | Budget)*, which also enjoys superb mountain vista. Hearty dishes from the grill and regional cuisine are served.

PONTA DO SOL (128 A 4) (𝄞 E–F 7)

Between two high rocky capes the town (pop. 4000, 3.5 km (2.2 mi) west of Ribeira Brava) rises from the sea to the sky. The old heart of the settlement consists of the church and a couple of dozen houses – and beyond that terraced fields of bananas. On the coastal strip a beach of grey stones fringes the bay, which draws the locals in summer. Two hotels have been built on the promenade, coffee shops welcome visitors, and the snack bar *Sol Poente (tel. 2 91 97 35 79)* perched on the cliffs offers simple meals with a view of the sea.

Villa Passos, a stately old house above the church, was the home of the grandfather of the American writer John Dos

In Ponta do Sol the church was built on the slope

Passos (Manhattan Transfer). In the 19th century he emigrated to the USA. A brass plaque commemorates the grandson's visit in 1960. The house and grounds have been restored; the *Centro Cultural John Dos Passos* was built in what used to be the garden. Accommodation is available in, for example, the *Estalagem da Ponta do Sol*, a minimalist modern development high up on the cliffs above the coast around a historic country house, with a pool and a cool bar *(54 rooms | Quinta da Rochinha | Caminho do Passo 6 | tel. 2 91 97 02 00 | www.pontadosol. com | Moderate)*.

THE NORTH

Between Porto Moniz and Porto da Cruz the island's rugged side becomes apparent: the coast is steeper, the ocean is wilder, a strong wind often blows, great waves come rolling in to delight surfers, and almost twice as much rain falls as in the south. However, there is a wealth of spectacular sights and experiences to make up for the weather.

A narrow cliff road winds along the coast, often right beside the waves. Nowadays bypass tunnels have been drilled through the rock in many places, but the drive is still an adventure – if only for the wonderful views and the waterfalls that tumble down from the heights. The scenery also features bizarrely shaped towers of rock and natural pools of lava that cooled and solidified thousands of years ago – and al-most everywhere walls have been added to them to make modern swimming pools. In some places terraces of vines cling to the rocky slopes, while elsewhere fertile valleys open a way into the heart of the island and climb up to the mountain ranges with their pointed rocky peaks, barren upland plateaus and jungles of laurisilva forest.

The inhabitants of the villages along the north coast lead a quiet life, almost independent of the world around them. For a long time they could reach the south only by sea or via paths across the mountains. This led to the emergence of strong, coherent village communities with all the facilities they needed to exist. Today tunnels connect them with Funchal, and many people commute there each day to their jobs. However, life in the villages has kept its ru-

Photo: Terraced fields in the Serra de Água

Crashing waves, wonderful views, pools in lava rock – the rugged north of Madeira is a fascinating landscape of adventure

ral character – and those who live here are not easily roused or flustered, not even by the tricks that the weather plays on the side of the island where the trade winds blow.

PORTO MONIZ

(121 D 1) (*ⅢⅢ C–D 1*) **Famous for its volcanic swimming pools, this pretty coastal community (pop. 1700) pulls**

in crowds of visitors in summer and at weekends – especially Madeirans.

Porto Moniz has now been smartened up, not only by renovating the *piscinas naturais,* which wind and waves formed over thousands of years. The harbour too has been extended, the old fort restored, a helicopter landing pad built and a new seafront promenade constructed. This promenade, the ● *Passeio Público Marítimo,* is the site of the modern science centre named *Centro Ciência Viva (admission 3.50 euros | Rotunda do Ilhéu Mole | www.ccvportomoniz.*

Lava pool: relax by the crashing surf

com) and the *Aquário da Madeira (admission 7 euros | Forte São João Batista | www.aquariodamadeira.com)* with more than 70 species of marine animals.

Settlement in Porto Moniz began around 1574, when Francisco Moniz, whom the king of Portugal had appointed to administer these lands, came to live here. Until the 19th century the town was a whaling station and trading port – and could only be reached by sea. The first coast road was not built until the mid-20th century.

The historic centre of Porto Moniz lies above the port, around the 17th-century church of *Nossa Senhora da Conceição*. If you arrive from Ponta do Pargo or Paúl da Serra, don't miss the superb view down to the coast from the ⊿ *Santinha* viewing point on the road above the town centre. A few bends before you get there, in *Lamaceiros*, a newly laid-out square with a mill, barbecue huts and toilets marks the starting point of the **INSIDER TIP** ▶ *Levada da Ribeira da Janela,* which flows 25 km (15.5 mi) to Fonte do Bispo.

FOOD & DRINK

PASTELARIA GAIVOTA

Excellent bakery, hearty local dishes and pizza. *Lugar do Tenente in the Gaivota Apartments building | tel. 2 91 85 00 40 | Budget*

SALGUEIRO

Fresh fish – with a sea view, in a rustic but contemporary ambience. *Lugar do Tenente 34 | tel. 2 91 85 00 80 | Moderate*

SWIMMING

Swimming in the ★ ● *lava pools:* in the centre of Porto Moniz the shallow pools, which gradually become deeper towards the sea, were reinforced with concrete and changing rooms were built *(all year | 1.25 euros).* A few paces from here by the *Cachalote* restaurant you can also take a dip in pools formed in volcanic rock, but there are no changing rooms. Bring along snorkelling gear to see the many fish that are washed over the wall into the lava pools at high tide

In the past these natural traps were used as a method of catching fish: the sap of a euphorbia plant that is poisonous to fish but harmless for humans was added to the water in the pool, so that the fish floated on the surface and could simply be collected. Today the pools are a poison-free and refreshing place to swim; on busy summer days sunbathers lie cheek by jowl on the concrete surfaces.

WHERE TO STAY

INSIDER TIP ► CASA DO RIBEIRINHO
A 100-year-old house between the sea and the mountains with beds for self-caterers. *Sítio do Ribeirinho | Santa do Porto Moniz | tel. 2 91 85 01 40 | www.moniztur. com | Budget*

MONIZ SOL ☺
Modern 3-star hotel with up-to-date design, very close to the harbour. Like the three other hotels of the Galoresort group, it complies with strict environmental standards. *47 rooms | tel. 2 91 85 01 50 | www.hotelmonizsol.com | Moderate*

INFORMATION

TOURIST INFORMATION
Opposite the piscinas naturais | tel. 2 91 85 25 55 | www.portomoniz.pt

WHERE TO GO

RIBEIRA DA JANELA (121 E 2) (𝑚 D 1)
In the course of millennia the water of this river, which flows into the ocean here, has carved out a magnificent, deeply cleft valley with rock walls that have a low cover of laurel woods in places. The ravine is an amazing sight. The village (pop. 300, 2 km (1.2 mi)

southeast of Porto Moniz) and the river take their name from a finger of rock in front of the river mouth, at the tip of which a window-like opening *(janela)* has been formed over the ages. At the edge of the village a road and the Levada dos Cedros lead inland to *Fanal* (121 E–F 4) *(𝑚 D–E 3)*, one of the most unspoilt and greenest parts of the island.

SANTANA

(124–125 C–D 3–4) (𝑚 L–M 2–3) Santana is the best-known town (pop. 3500) on the north coast, thanks to its old wooden thatched houses.
About 100 of these ★ *casas de colmo* still exist in and around the town. A few of them have been reconstructed next to the modern town hall; behind its colourful façade one contains original furnishings and a craft workshop, for example for linen weaving, and another houses the tourist office. Anyone who is reminded of ● Asterix and Obelix at

★ **Lava pools**
Swimming among the volcanic rocks – natural pools in Porto Moniz → p. 62

★ **Casas de colmo**
Thatched and brightly coloured: almost like the world of Asterix and Obelix → p. 63

★ **Pico Ruivo**
Madeira's highest summit is accessible to walkers → p. 65

★ **Grutas de São Vicente**
Take a walk into the bowels of the island → p. 67

MARCO POLO HIGHLIGHTS

SANTANA

Living history: casas de colmo in Santana

the sight of these brightly coloured little houses is not far wide off the mark: they probably have a Celtic origin. Families occupied them until a few decades ago, living here in extremely spartan conditions. In the lower room there was space for a bed, a seat and a washbasin. Children slept under the pointed roof, which could only be reached from outside, through a skylight. Family life took place mainly outside the house. Today a few *casas de colmo* have extensions and are still occupied.

Below the church of Santana a sign points to the INSIDER TIP ▶ *Rocha do Navio*, a nature reserve established to protect endemic coastal plants and rare sea birds. On Wednesdays and at the weekend a lift runs several times a day for the farmers, also transporting holidaymakers *(return trip 5 euros/from the cliff down to the tiny beach, next to which there are a few little fields)*. Santana is also home to the *Parque Temático da Madeira*, which is devoted to the history and culture of the island. Its pavilions also take up the theme of the future of the earth *(daily 10am–7pm, closed Mon off-season | admission 10 euros | Fonte da Pedra | www.parquetematicodama deira.pt)*.

FOOD & DRINK

O PESCADOR
Comfortable modern eatery with an emphasis on fish and seafood – e.g. *saltimbocca de tamboril*. *Pico António Fernandes | tel. 2 91 57 22 72 | Moderate*

RESTAURANTE RANCHO MADEIRENSE
Filling meals from the grill with the atmosphere of riding stables on the way to Pico Ruivo. *Pico das Pedras | tel. 2 91 57 02 30 | Moderate*

WHERE TO STAY

INSIDER TIP CASAS DO CAMPO DO POMAR

Quinta estate above the village with four studios, three cottages and three rooms in the main house. *Sítio do Lombo do Curral | tel. 2 91 57 00 70 | www.proteas-pomar. com | Budget*

O COLMO

What used to be the basic Residencial in the village centre has become a modern mid-range hotel with thatched houses in the courtyard, a swimming pool and a cosy atmosphere. *43 rooms | Sítio do Serrado | tel. 2 91 57 02 90 | www.hotelo-colmo.com | Budget–Moderate*

INFORMATION

TOURIST INFORMATION
Sítio do Serrado | tel. 2 91 57 29 92

WHERE TO GO

FAIAL (125 E 4–5) (*ωω M–N 3*)
Amidst terraces of vines and orchards this charming village of 2000 residents, 9 km (5.6 mi) southeast of Santana, nestles at the foot of a 600-metre mountain by the sea – the *Penha de Águia* ('Eagle Rock'). Ospreys are said to have nested there, and seen from the right angle its western flank looks like a bird's head – hence the name. From the ☼ summit the view along the north coast is splendid.

If the prospect of trout in bacon with a mountain of vegetables and sweet potatoes sounds enticing, stop at the *Casa de Chá do Faial (Lombo do Baixo | tel. 2 915722 23 | Moderate)*. The locals as well as tour operators appreciate this restaurant with its furnishings of wood and basketwork. Go up to the ☼ INSIDER TIP roof terrace for a great panorama.

PICO RUIVO ★ ☼
(124 A–B 6) (*ωω K 4*)
Madeira's highest mountain (1862 m, 2036 yd), 10 km (6.2 mi) southwest of Santana, is the finishing point of a wonderful hike via Achada do Teixeira. If the weather is kind, the panorama from the wooden platform at the summit is breathtaking. The ascent to the peak on a paved path is not difficult and takes no more than one hour. Along the way the Ruivos mountain refuge offers refreshments. Walkers who are fit and well equipped can press on to the 1818-metre *Pico do Arieiro (130 B 2) (ωω K 5)*. In early summer a unique display of endemic alpine flowers can be seen here. In very dry summers, as in August 2010, this vegetation is affected by forest fires, but the wet winter climate enables it to recover fairly quickly.

PORTO DA CRUZ (125 F 5) (*ωω N 4*)
The port (porto) of the cross (cruz) that was erected by the first inhabitants is one of the oldest settlements on the island, today with a population of 3000, 12 km (7.5 mi) southeast of Santana. A beach promenade and pools for swimmers have made the town smarter and up to date. One of Madeira's few remaining sugar-cane mills stands on the promontory between two beaches of black lava sand. There are also atmospheric wine cellars here, some of them almost 400 years old.

For a good old-fashioned place to eat, try the little *snack bar A Pipa (Casas Próximas | mobile tel. 9 68 52 74 00)*, where guests are treated to hearty meals with ingredients from the sea and mountains. For those who want to stay overnight here, the modern *Costa Linda (13 rooms | Rua João Abel de Freitas | tel. 2 91 56 00 80 | www.costa-linda.net | Budget–Moderate)* is recommended.

QUEIMADAS (124 C 5) (*M L 3*)

From the car park of the *Rancho Madeirense* holiday village (on the road to Pico das Pedras) a shady path leads along a levada and through green laurel woodland to the *Queimadas forest lodge*. The walk of just under an hour is also suitable for people with impaired sight, as the route has been enclosed with wooden fencing and laid out as a INSIDER TIP *path for the blind*. From Santana a narrow lane leads 4.5 km (2.8 mi) up to a former charcoal-burners' settlement. This is a picturesque spot at an altitude of 900 m in a clearing surrounded by rhododendrons and has an area with ponds and picnic table. Queimadas is the starting point for a variety of walking trails, for example to the ☙ *Levada do Caldeirão Verde*. With fantastic coastal views this levada runs to the Madeira Nature Park via the *Caldeirão Verde*, a little green lake fed by a waterfall.

SÃO JORGE (124 C 2–3) (*M L 2*)

The main attraction of the village (pop. 1700, 6 km (3.7 mi) northwest of Santana) is the ● *Igreja de São Jorge*. With its gilded Baroque carvings and 18th-century tiled frieze this parish church is regarded as the most beautiful and artistically valuable place of worship in the north of the island. Directly behind the church a typical rectangular thatched house harbours a little restaurant, *Casa de Palha* (*Achada Grande* | *tel. 2 91 57 63 82* | *Budget*), where diners are served skilfully prepared regional dishes. Don't fail to try the *consomé de camarão no pão,* a creamy shrimp soup in a bread bowl. From the church a road leads to the ☙ *Ponta de São Jorge*, jutting into the sea with its lighthouse *(farol)*. From the old foresters' lookout ☙ INSIDER TIP *Ponta Vigia* near the lighthouse you can enjoy the coastal views undisturbed.

☙ *Cabana* on the road to Arco de São Jorge affords a dizzying vantage point. Farmers often sell tropical fruit here to tourists who come to take photos. Shortly before reaching Arco de São Jorge, flower-lovers should stop at the *rose garden (Roseiral)* of the *Quinta do Arco*, where more than 1700 kinds of roses are grown (*daily 10am–6pm* | *admission 5 euros* | *Sítio da Lagoa* | *tel. 2 91 57 02 50* | *www.quintadoarco.com*). On the same grounds, fans of wine will be interested by the little *Museu do Vinho e da Vinha (closed Sun/Mon* | *admission 2 euros)*. For a leisurely afternoon tea or a hearty meal, the *Casa de Chá Quinta do Arco (tel. 2 91 57 81 85* | *Moderate)* is recommended.

SÃO VICENTE

(122–123 C–D 4–5) (〰 G–H 3) **Prettied up in the 1980s with the help of EU funds, this showcase village for the north of Madeira with 3400 residents now holds an award for conservation.** Its neat whitewashed houses with a few shops and restaurants nestle in the alleys and stepped paths around the parish church.

GRUTAS DE SÃO VICENTE ★

At the southern edge of São Vicente the Grutas de São Vicente illustrate the geological history of Madeira. A system of lava tunnels with a length of approx. 700 m (765 yd), which was created by a volcanic eruption 890,000 years ago and was first explored in the late 19th century, has been made accessible to the public. The addition of a modern pavilion, the ● *Centro do Vulcanismo*, enables visitors to take a virtual journey into the geo-

A journey into the volcano: the Grutas de São Vicente

SIGHTSEEING

CAPELINHA DO CALHAU

In 1692 a striking little chapel dedicated to St Vincent was built into the rock that stands where the Ribeira de São Vicente flows into the sea. Mosaics made with pebbles from the beach adorn the Baroque façade.

logical heart of Madeira and learn about volcanic activity all over the world *(tours in English daily 10am–7pm | admission caves and pavilion 8 euros | Sítio do pé do Passo | www.grutasecentrodovulcanismo. com)*. On the grounds there is also a *botanical park* with almost all the endemic coastal plants that grown on the island *(free admission)*.

SÃO VICENTE

IGREJA DE SÃO VICENTE
The sanctuary and side altars of this 18th-century church are decorated with the gilded carvings *(talha dourada)* typical of Portuguese Baroque. A beautiful azulejo frieze adorns the walls, and the painting on the ceiling of the nave shows St Vincent blessing the village that bears his name.

FOOD & DRINK

FERRO VELHO
Traditional regional and international food in a rustic environment. Nice location in the small pedestrian zone with a cosy terrace. *Rua da Fonte Velha | tel. 2 91 84 27 63 | Budget–Moderate*

QUEBRA MAR
This typically Madeiran restaurant serves local and international fish and meat dishes. Try the filling fish soup and *carne vinho e alhos,* beef in garlic and wine sauce. *Sítio do Calhau | tel. 2 91 84 23 38 | Budget–Moderate*

WHERE TO STAY

CASA DA CAMÉLIA
Two basic two-storey cottages on private land; the common kitchen in a separate building has lots of character. *4 rooms | Sítio do Poiso | tel. 2 91 84 22 06 | Budget*

SOLAR DA BICA
Well-kept modern country house above the village centre in the direction of the Encumeada Tunnel. *14 rooms | Sítio dos Lameiros | tel. 2 91 84 20 18 | www.solardabica.pt | Budget–Moderate*

WHERE TO GO

PONTA DELGADA (123 E 3) (ⅉ H–J 2)
Once a year this normally sleepy village (pop. 1400, 7 km (4.3 mi) east of São Vicente) is inundated with visitors: on the first Sunday in September, when pilgrims come to pay respect to the wooden figure of Senhor Bom Jesus, a crucifix that is said to have been washed up here in the 15th century in a chest. The church that was erected on the spot where it was found burned down almost completely in 1908, and the flames spread to the crucifix too. The charred remains of it were saved, and are kept in a glass case in the new church, which is decorated in the Baroque style.

Take the ⚴ path that leads around the apse to enjoy a fine view towards the coast near São Jorge. The *Monte Mar Palace (111 rooms | tel. 2 91 86 00 30 | www.*

LONELY PEAKS

Madeira and Porto Santo are no more than the tips of a gigantic range of volcanic mountains whose foundations lie at a depth of more than 4000 m. 10–20 million years ago they emerged from the Atlantic breakers following a series of eruptions. Volcanic activity continued on the archipelago until about 2000 years ago. The course of the streams of lava and the sites of lava stacks are still clearly recognisable in some places on Madeira: in and around Porto Moniz, between Pico do Arieiro and Pico Ruivo, between Fajã da Ovelha and Jardim do Mar and in the caves of São Vicente.

montemar-palace.com | *Moderate)* hotel above the cliffs boasts a seawater pool, a health club, sauna, and courts for tennis and squash. A more intimate alternative to this luxury accommodation is situated 2 km (1.2 mi) away among terraces of vines and vegetables in the village of *Boaventura.* The *Solar da Boaventura (30 rooms | Sítio do Serrão | tel. 2 91 86 08 88 | www.solar-boaventura.com | Budget)*, an 18th-century house with a cosy, rustic atmosphere, a modern annexe and excellent food is a stylish place to stay.

ROSÁRIO (123 D 5) (*ⱷ G–H 4*)

4 km (2.5 mi) south of São Vicente a lonely bell tower stands on a hill. In the 1950s the congregation built this chapel, which consists of no more than the walls of the tower, to honour the Virgin of Fátima.

SEIXAL (122 A 3) (*ⱷ E 2*)

Seixal is 7.5 km (4.7 mi) west of São Vicente. The houses of this hamlet of around 800 residents can be seen from afar, radiant on a rocky headland. Almost every one of them has a garden full of vines, growing grapes which are sold each autumn to make Madeira wine. The first mention of Seixal in documents dates from 1553. The villagers had built a chapel dedicated to São Antão, the patron of livestock. In the 18th century the chapel was enlarged and, as was usual in those days, the local fishermen paid for the construction by donating half of their catch. If you drive west from the church you pass a signpost to the *piscina*, the seawater pool. In the harbourside *Restaurante Brisa Mar (Cais do Seixal | tel. 2 91 85 44 76 | Budget–Moderate)* the fish comes straight out of the sea onto the plate. A bed for the night can be had in the attached *Estalagem (12 rooms | www.brisa-mar.com)* or in *Casa das Videiras (4 rooms | Sítio da Serra d'Água |*

Lilies fringe the path to the Fátima Chapel of Rosário

tel. 2 91 22 26 67 | www.casa-das-videiras. com | Budget), a country house on the slopes of the Serra de Água.

At the eastern end of Seixal a lane climbs up to *Chão da Ribeira*, where the *Casa de Pasto (tel. 2 91 85 45 59 | Budget–Moderate)* dishes up fresh trout and delicious skewered beef. On the road from Seixal to São Vicente the ☆ *Véu da Noiva* lookout commands a stunning view of the northern coast.

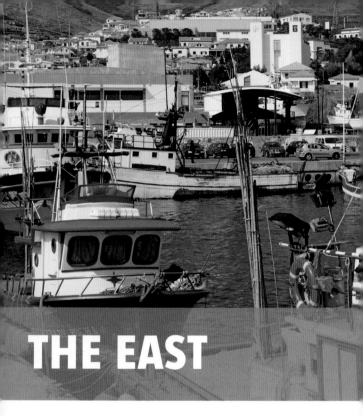

THE EAST

The east of Madeira is more varied than any other part of the island. Cool green uplands contrast with bare, desert-like earth, and contemporary architecture is coupled with traditional sites of ancient crafts.

The eastern part of the island, between Gaula and Ponta de São Lourenço, also has a richer history than some other regions. Explorers, pirates and eloped lovers anchored off this coast, whalers went about their bloody business and rich merchants built lavish summer residences. Today the modern, extended Santa Catarina international airport and Machico, the island's third-largest town, mark the scene. Further evidence of the speed of progress is apparent in the new cargo port at Caniçal, the sports facilities near the airport and the marina development at Quinta do Lorde. Thanks to fast road connections on the *Via Rápida*, the modern face of Madeira has come to the east: many residents commute from Santa Cruz or Machico to their jobs in Funchal, as the new fast highway, low prices for accommodation and an increasing range of leisure amenities have persuaded many people to live here. In Machico a new scene for party people is emerging, and many residents of Funchal are happy to make the trip to Caniçal to dine in several high-quality restaurants. Rural areas of small farming villages are situated in the mountains above the coastal settlements. Old Madeira can still be found here – and therefore many places to eat and drink in the typical island style. This

Photo: Fishing boats in the harbour of Caniçal

Plenty of history and contrasts – the east of the island is where the first explorers landed, and where projects for the future are emerging

region is known for especially generous portions of skewered meat dishes and strong *poncha*.

CAMACHA

(131 E 4) *(ⓜ N 7)* **This town of 8000 inhabitants occupies a flat hilltop 700 m above sea level.**

Camacha is surrounded by terraced fields of apple trees, whose fruit is made into sparkling *cidra*, and moist valleys. On the valley bottoms grow the small basket willows from which the people of Camacha make furniture and other kinds of basketwork. About one third of the residents madke a living from this craft, and usually the whole family is involved in basket weaving. In spring the men cut willow twigs, which are then boiled or soaked for several weeks. Heating the willow – this produces a pungent smell – lends it a red-brown colour. Basket weaving is a cottage industry, and if you ask around a little, you will certainly be able to get

A woven zoo in Café Relógio: a matter of taste

brought a ball with him from home and organised two teams. A modern monument in the municipal park commemorates this event. The 'industrialisation' of basket weaving in Camacha is also owed to the initiative of a few Englishmen who frequented Camacha in the 19th century as an upland summer resort. They commissioned the locals, who until then had mainly produced baskets for transport, to make furniture from woven willow – which was then a fashionable kind of furnishing in England. Soon these elaborate works of craftsmanship became an important export item for Madeira. Nowadays cheap competition from Asia makes life hard for the island's basket weavers.

FOOD & DRINK

CASA DE PASTO O BOLEO
Old-style restaurant at the edge of the church square with a changing daily menu of Madeiran dishes and a small terrace on the road. *Sítio da Igreja | tel. 2 91 92 21 28 | Budget–Moderate*

SHOPPING

CAFÉ RELÓGIO
Behind the façade of what used to be a British summer residence with its clock tower is Madeira's largest basketwork store, which has become a must for the tourist trade: coaches and chauffeured taxi tours never fail to stop here. A workshop for demonstrating the craft has been set up in the cellar of this multi-storey building, where everything from bottles in woven willow to laundry baskets can be found on the shelves. Although a good many products belong to the realm of kitsch, it is also possible to find attractive and useful souvenirs here. *Daily 9am–6pm | Largo da Achada | www. caferelogio.com*

the address of one of the INSIDER TIP studios of the *vimeiros* (*vimes* means gorse or broom).
Failing that, the place to go for basketware is *Café Relógio* on the broad, green main square of Camacha, *Largo da Achada*, where the first football match on Portuguese territory was played in 1875. A British citizen who lived in Camacha

WHERE TO STAY

CASAS VALLEPARAIZO
Eight holiday homes in typical Madeiran style with a total of 20 rooms in gardens in a picturesque valley close to Camacha. *Estrada Regional 102, no. 161 | tel. 2 91 92 21 74 | mobile tel. 9 62 93 93 57 | www.valleparaizo.com | Moderate*

WHERE TO GO

PARQUE ECOLÓGICO DO FUNCHAL ☺
(130–131 B–D 1–3) *(ℳ M 6)*
Between Monte, the Pico do Arieiro, the Poiso Pass and Camacha, a nature reserve covering an area of almost 1000 ha has been the site of reforestation projects since 1994. In the *Centro de Recepção e Interpretação (Estrada Regional 103 no. 259 | between Monte and Poiso-Pass | daily 9am–5.30pm),* in addition to a little café there are information displays about the flora and fauna, regular workshops and courses in environmental studies for school classes and other interested persons. The park authority is also active in installing playgrounds, picnic places, walking trails and educational materials. In summer 2010 a good deal of the park was destroyed in forest fires, since when the reforestation and building of infrastructure has started all over again. One activity on offer is a INSIDER TIP donkey ride in the park *(5 euros/15 min, ask at the information centre or call tel. 291 78 31 34 | mobile tel. 917 44 39 33).*

PASSO DO POISO (131 D 3) *(ℳ M 6)*
Roads from all four points of the compass meet at the top of the pass, which is located 10 km (6.2 mi) northwest of Camacha at an elevation of 1400 m (1,530 yd). From here you can drive up to the Pico do Arieiro, across to Santo da Serra, down to Funchal and also to Faial.

What was once a shepherd's shelter at the crossroads has recently been turned into a popular rustic *restaurant*, where the spicy bread soup called *açorda* and juicy beef skewers are served in front of a crackling open fire *(Casa de Abrigo do Poiso | noon–midnight | tel. 2 91 78 22 69 | Budget–Moderate).*

RIBEIRO FRIO ● (131 D 1) *(ℳ M 5)*
On the 'cold stream', a few hairpin bends to the north of the Poiso Pass, 14 km (8.7 mi) northwest of Camacha, the state forestry organisation has set up a trout farm and created a little botanical garden with camellias and laurel shrubs around the fish ponds, which are filled with water from the stream. Thanks to an ingenious system of sluices along the slope, the fish move from one pond to another as they increase in size, until finally enormous trout can be admired in a large round pool. There are no prizes for guessing what's on the menu not far away at the *Restaurante Ribeiro Frio*, also known as *Victor's Bar (9am–7pm | tel. 2 91 57 58 98 | Budget–Moderate)*: fresh and smoked trout.

Behind the restaurant is access to the ☙ ● *Levada do Furado*, which sure-footed walkers can follow for some 11 km (6.8 mi), with wonderful views of

★ **Museu da Baleia**
The whaling museum in Caniçal tells the story of whales and how they were hunted from Madeira
→ p. 76

★ **Ponta de São Lourenço**
The eastern tip of Madeira – a wonderful experience for hikers → p. 77

MARCO POLO HIGHLIGHTS

the north coast all the way, as far as the Portela Pass. If all you want is to take a short walk, look out on the road for a yellow sign marked 'Balcões'. From here it takes about 30 minutes to reach the ☀ viewing point of that name.

MACHICO

(132 B–C 3) (*𝓜 P 5–6*) **In the broad fertile valley of the Machico river, Madeira's third-largest town (pop. 12,000) spreads from the coast up to the mountain slopes.**

The first settlement on the island, it was founded by the explorer João Gonçalves Zarco, who set anchor in the bay in 1419 after arriving from Porto Santo with his followers Tristão Vaz Teixeira and Bartolomeu Perestrelo. According to a legend, however, the town originated when a pair of English lovers, Anne Dorset and Robert Machyn, were stranded here before Zarco's time.

Machico prospered as early as the 15th century from the cultivation of sugar cane and for a few decades was even the capital of the northeastern part of the island, until Funchal gained the role of sole capital of Madeira in 1497. Machico then drifted into a kind of deep slumber, from which it did not awake until a few decades ago. Today the town has a good deal to be proud of, and many investments, especially in the redevelopment of the waterfront, have come to fruition today. There are plenty of reasons to visit Machico, which is split into two halves by the river.

BANDA D'ALÉM

The historic fishermen's quarter lies on the east bank of the Ribeira da Machico. Where once ships' carpenters made wooden boats in a little shipyard there is a now a new marina with a few pleasant cafés and restaurants. In summer visitors flock to the **INSIDER TIP** new beach of bright sand, which was made by im-

In Machico they take their dominoes seriously – and onlookers are tolerated

porting sand from Africa and is protected by a pier.

CAPELA DOS MILAGRES

Largo dos Milagres, a square shaded by tall ficus trees, is the place where the first church on Madeira was built back in the year 1420. The 'chapel of miracles' that stands there today dates from 1810. The previous building fell victim to disastrous floods, with the exception of the coat of arms on its gable and a doorway with a pointed arch. Fishermen miraculously salvaged the statue of Christ, which had been swept out to sea by the floods. A painting to the left of the altar depicts this event.

FORTS

In the 18th century the people of Machico tried to protect their easily accessible bay from pirate raids by constructing three forts. Two of them have survived: the *Forte de São João Baptista* to the east, which is not open to the public, and the triangular *Forte de Nossa Senhora do Amparo,* now the tourist information office. It is just a stone's throw from the latter to the newly developed promenade, between the new complex of the multipurpose *Forum Machico* and the mouth of the Machico river.

NOSSA SENHORA DA CONCEIÇÃO

The main parish church dates back to the 15th century. King Manuel I donated the side doorway with its three marble columns. The main portal too still has its decorative work from the Manueline period: grotesque faces that symbolise good and evil. As the interior of the church was thoroughly remodelled during the Baroque era, only the two side chapels hint at its original appearance. One of them displays the coat of arms of the Teixeira family. A statue of Tristão

Vaz Teixeira, who ruled the eastern part of Madeira from Machico, stands on the square in front of the church.

Diagonally opposite is the *town hall,* which was built in the early 20th century. Here both coats of arms of the town can be seen: the historic version, reportedly granted in 1499 by King Manuel I in the form of an armillary sphere, an astronomic instrument of that time, and the version chosen in the mid-20th century with an irrigation canal and two sugarcane plants.

FOOD & DRINK

BAÍA

Popular place in the new marina with a large terrace overlooking the water. The specialities are fish and seafood. Karaoke at weekends. *Porto de Recreio | tel. 2 91 96 65 02 | Moderate*

INSIDER TIP MERCADO VELHO

Likeable restaurant in (and in front of) the old market building. Recommended not only for lunch but also for coffee and a cake in the afternoon. *Rua do Mercado | tel. 2 91 96 59 26 | Moderate*

O GALÃ

Something between a bar, bakery and restaurant. Local dishes at reasonable prices. *Rua General António Teixeira de Aguiar 1–7 | tel. 2 91 96 57 20 | Budget–Moderate*

WHERE TO STAY

HOTEL DOM PEDRO BAÍA CLUB

Modern high-rise hotel on the western side of the bay with a diving station, tennis court, tropical garden and big pool area. *218 rooms | Estrada de São Roque | tel. 2 91 96 95 00 | www.dompedro.com | Moderate*

MACHICO

RESIDENCIAL AMPARO
Modern guesthouse near the Amparo fort. Its *restaurant* dishes up treats such as *espada* covered with shrimps and melted cheese. *12 rooms | Rua da Amargura | tel. 2 91 96 81 20 | www.residencialamparo. web.pt | Budget*

INFORMATION

TOURIST INFORMATION
Forte Nossa Senhora do Amparo | tel. 2 91 96 22 89

WHERE TO GO

CANIÇAL (132–133 C–D 2) (*∅ Q 5*)
For a long time fishing, whaling and boat building put their stamp on Madeira's easternmost town (pop. 4000), 7 km (4.3 mi) northeast of Machico. Today the large free-trade zone and the cargo port dominate the life of this rapidly growing community. For a reminder of Caniçal's past as a major whaling station visit the modern ★ ● *Museu da Baleia (free admission | Rua Pedra d'Eira | www. museudabaleia.org)*. This museum has information about the impressive sperm whales that were hunted and presents the history of whaling on Madeira, which continued until the 1980s, and the stages of the whaling business from manual harpooning from little rowing boats to the processing of the catch.

For a snack, stop at *Muralha's Bar (tel. 2 91 96 14 68 | Budget)* opposite the new swimming pool, which has bags of character and mainly serves fish. It's one of the places where you can sometimes get INSIDER TIP *castanhetas*, small fish like anchovies. Some more bars and restaurants are strung out along the new harbour road as far as the shipyard or cargo terminal. A bit further east the yachting crowd like to moor in the modern, boldly designed *Quinta do Lorde* marina, where there are bars and a restaurant *(www. quintadolorde.pt)*.

In 1986 the sea near Caniçal was declared a ☺ *marine nature reserve*. This ensures that not only different whale species but also dolphins and the highly endangered monk seals can live undisturbed in these waters.

PICO DO FACHO ☇ (132 C 3) (*∅ P 5*)
To the east of Machico (approx. 4.5 km, 2.8 mi) a narrow road leads up to Pico do Facho, where the summit at 322 m commands an outstanding view south towards the bay of Machico and the airport and northeast towards the harbours of Caniçal and Ponta de São Lourenço. At weekends the hill is a much-loved picnic spot frequented by Madeiran families. 'Beacon Hill' takes its name from the fires that lookouts lit up there in bygone days to give warning of impending pirate attacks.

LOW BUDGET

▶ If you ask persistently, the *tourist office* in *Machico* provides addresses for private rooms in and around the town that are not officially indexed. An overnight stay usually costs less then 25 euros. For a central location at an unbeatable price, consider the 11 basic rooms at the *Residencial O Facho | Praçeta 25 Abril | Machico | tel. 2 91 96 27 86*

▶ On the *Sunday market* in *Santo da Serra* you will find stalls with clothes, fruit and vegetables, but also a large area with snack stands and grills where you can eat much more cheaply than in the local restaurants.

PONTA DE SÃO LOURENÇO ★
(133 D–F 2) (*𝑚 Q–S 5*)

The eastern tip of Madeira, 11 km (6.8 mi) from Machico, is barren and windy. Clearing of the forest cover began here at an early date, and later the land was used to pasture goats, which immediately devoured any green shoots. As a result the landscape is now a scene of bare hills,

Below the ☼ Baía de Abra you can look across to the *Ilhas Desertas.* Only a few metres of water separate the Ponta de São Lourenço from two islets, the *Ilhéu de Agostinho* and the *Ilhéu de Fora.* The latter is popularly known as *Ilhéu do Farol*, as Madeira's oldest lighthouse has occupied the summit since 1870. The islands are accessible only for scientific

At Ponta de São Lourenço the coast drops almost vertically into the sea

which are carpeted in flowers in spring, and bizarrely shaped rocks that rise from the turquoise sea, as if piled up by the hands of children, in the colours of ochre, rust-red, grey and greenish-black.

There is a ☼ picnic spot with a wonderful view of the sea and the headland at *Ponta do Rosto.* The road leading to Ponta de São Lourenço ends at a car park for walkers above the *Baía de Abra.* The walk to the eastern tip of the island and back reveals new scenic vistas at every twist and turn of the track.

research. For the finest view of these offshore islands and the lighthouse, go to the twin peaks of the 125 m (137 yd) ☼ *Ponta do Furado,* the 'pierced tip', as this hill is known thanks to holes that the sea has carved out of its rocks. The ascent is very steep, but spectacular views are the reward.

PORTELA (131 F 1) (*𝑚 N 5*)

This village, strung out along the road 9 km (5.6 mi) northwest of Machico, marks the island's watershed. Its centre consists of a taxi rank, a bus stop and a ☀ viewpoint with a rustic restaurant, the ● *Miradouro da Portela (tel. 2 9196 6169 | Budget)*. From here the view across to the 'eagle rock' Penha de Águia on the north coast is stunning. To the left, some way behind the flower stalls, is the start of the themed 'path for all' (12.5 km, 7.8 mi) to *Fajã dos Rolos*, which is suitable for wheelchairs, cyclists and walkers.

SANTO DA SERRA (132 A 3) (*ぬ O 5–6*)

Long before Robert Trent Jones designed Madeira's first gold course at Santo da Serra (more precisely: at Santo António da Serra), many visitors came to the attractive, usually fresh and breezy hilly country 8.5 km (5.3 mi) west of Machico in which this village (pop. 1400) nestles. Sugar magnates and other wealthy Madeirans built their summer homes here. Among them were the Blandy family, wine merchants who came to the island from England. Their estate, the *Quinta do Santo da Serra* near the church, is now public land, and the Madeirans love to come to its garden for a picnic. A little zoo with ponies, deer and stags is attached. At the rear of the garden the ☀ *Miradouro dos Ingleses* has a panoramic view of the east of the island. The Blandys once posted lookouts here to watch the shipping that approached Madeira.

Snacks and meat skewers are on the menu in the rustic *A Nossa Aldeia* restaurant *(Sítio dos Casais Próximos | tel. 2 9155 2142 | Budget)*. For an overnight stay, the right address is the sky-blue *Quinta Serra Golf (22 rooms | Casais Próximos | tel. 2 9155 05 00 | www.serragolf. com | Moderate)*, stylish surroundings that can be enjoyed over `INSIDER TIP` afternoon tea.

SANTA CRUZ

(132 A–B 4–5) (ぬ O–P 6–7) **Although one of Madeira's oldest settlement, this coastal town of 6000 inhabitants is hardly visited by tourists.**

Which is a pity, because Santa Cruz is an attractive place with gardens and narrow alleys. In the centre stands the church of *São Salvador*, which dates back to 1533 and, like the town hall on the edge of town, has stone carvings from the Manueline period. In the choir is the tomb of João de Freitas, a feudal lord who commissioned the building of the church for

THE HEALING FLOWER

'Sometimes my mother would cut off one of the fleshy leaves and lay it on little scrapes and wounds,' says Dona Maria. For generations many Madeirans have known and prized the healing properties of aloe vera, which grows everywhere on the island and blooms yellow once a year. The plant, which is also known as the 'desert lily', is cultivated on the south coast but also around Seixal in the north, and demand is growing steadily. Three times a year the island's farmers can harvest three arms of the plant. They are then pulverised and exported, or processed in a workshop on the spot, usually to make cosmetics. White tubes and phials with a picture of the aloe are available in supermarkets, pharmacies and some of the better souvenir shops on Madeira.

this community, which had grown rich from sugar exports.

A 20th-century Portuguese artist, Out-eiro Águeda, did the frieze of tiles on the INSIDER TIP market hall (Mon/Sat 7am–4pm, Tue–Thu 7am–7pm, Sun 7am–1pm), which has a good reputation for its range of freshly caught fish. The frieze depicts a variety of agricultural labours and the work of the fishermen and fishmongers. A few yards behind the market hall is the long grey pebbly beach of Santa Cruz, next to which a row of date palms wave their fronds in the breeze and a recently renovated *promenade* invites visitors to take a stroll.

FOOD & DRINK

MARISQUERIA SÁ MAR

All the bounty of the sea finds its way into the kitchen here, from dried cod to limpets and the catch of the day. *Rua Bela de São José 19 | tel. 2 91 52 42 33 | Budget*

ACTIVITIES & SPORTS

At the eastern end of the beach below a wall of black rock there is a pool, the *Praia das Palmeiras*. In *Ribeira da Boaventura* a new swimming *complex* has been built with convenient access to the sea via a sheltered little bay between the area for water sports and the two swimming pools. A further attraction is the new *Aquapark* in Santa Cruz, which boasts pools, water chutes and all sorts of other fun.

WHERE TO STAY

RESIDENCIAL SANTO ANTÓNIO

This B & B is popular with walkers. It is simply styled and has a small restaurant, a mere 75 m from the beach. *14 rooms |*

Santa Cruz: fishing boat beneath a date palm

Rua Cónego César de Oliveira | tel. 2 91 52 41 98 | www.residencialsantoantonio.com.pt | Budget

INFORMATION

CÂMARA MUNICIPAL DE SANTA CRUZ

Town hall: Largo do Município | tel. 2 91 52 01 00 | www.cm-santacruz.pt

PORTO SANTO

Dourada, 'the golden one', is what the people of Porto Santo call their island. Almost 9 km (5.6 mi) of bright fine-grained sand on the south coast live up to this name – and so does the caramel-coloured earth, which puts on a thin veil of green only in spring.

Otherwise naked rock is the dominant feature of Madeira's dry little sister – which is proud of being the first island of the archipelago that was discovered. Just a few thousand trees cling with their roots to several conical mountains – the first fruits of a forestation programme that began some time ago, after the revolution of 1974, and has now been adapted to the local conditions thanks to its own tree nursery and professional methods of planting (by hand!).

Today it is almost inconceivable that forests of dragon trees once thrived, and later fields of corn swayed in the wind on the island, which is 11 km (6.8 mi) long and 6 km (3.7 mi) wide. Only a few years after a storm drove the Portuguese knights João Gonçalves Zarco and Tristão Vaz Teixeira to the coast of the previously undiscovered Porto Santo, the little island was being used as a supply station for seafarers undertaking long voyages. Christopher Columbus was one of the first of them when in 1478 he landed on Madeira, though still in the role of a sugar merchant at that time. A little later, according to legend, he married Felipa Moniz, the daughter of Bartolomeu Perestrelo, who was the first captain legate (a kind of governor) of Porto Santo at that time.

Photo: Sandy beach at Vila Baleira

The beauty of sand and rock – the charms of Madeira's island neighbour are miles of beach, crystal-clear ocean waters and lots of action

In the 16th century Spanish and Italian merchants discovered the riches that lay in the dragon-tree forests of Porto Santo: the resin of this palm-like plant was greatly coveted in Europe as a dye for textiles and lacquer. The merchants therefore went to work vigorously, and bled the trunks of the dragon trees dry. This ruthless exploitation, but also forest clearance by fire and excessive pasturing, destroyed the island vegetation over a period of time. The soil dried out, and fertile earth was washed into the Atlantic by the wind and rain. Much later the construction of a Nato air base swallowed up more agricultural land. Now the terraced fields on which fruit and vegetables were grown well into the 20th century largely lie fallow and the villages are in a state of decay.

Almost all of the 4500 inhabitants of Porto Santo live on the south coast now. Tourism has evolved as the main pillar of the economy. The visitors are for the most part Portuguese citizens from the European mainland, and Madeirans

An idealised portrayal: Columbus in bronze

too. In the peak season between July and September prices go through the roof: a hotel room costs twice as much in these months as in April or October. To compensate for this there is a lot going on – from a beach volleyball tournament to music and dance events. Outside the months when the Portuguese take their holidays, by contrast, the island goes back to sleep – even though it has a pleasant temperate climate almost all year round, and wonderful rock formations can be admired there at any time. The tourism strategists are planning to change this situation, however, with the help of a broadly sweeping 18-hole golf course, which will be extended to the north by a further nine holes, and by improved marketing of the hydrotherapy treatment spa facilities and the sand, which is considered to have healing properties for rheumatism and other complaints. The regional government found out to its cost that not every large-scale tourism project is a success when the investor behind the gigantic *Colombo Beach Resorts* became insolvent. For years now this five-star complex by the coast near to Vila Baleira has been half-finished and awaits completion. On the other hand the luxury hotel *Pestana Porto Santo (275 rooms | tel. 2 91 14 40 00 | www.pestana-porto-santo.com | Expensive)*, which attracts guests with its outstanding spa, has already opened. Further signs of planned change are evident in the extensions to the road Networks, the new *Zarco Shopping Center* beside the beach zone and a newly built bike track between Vila Baleira and Ponta da Calheta.

VILA BALEIRA

(135 D 3–4) (*V–W 11*) As befits its size (pop. 2600), the capital of the island has all the charm of a village.

This applies at least to the historic centre of Vila Baleira with its white houses, in whose shade sunburnt old men sit to pay dominoes and a colourful mix of people meet for a cup of coffee.

About half of the island's residents have their homes in its miniature metropolis by the harbour, where there are at least a few banks and supermarkets. In summer the number of people crowding into this tranquil place is many times higher, especially on *Largo do Pelourinho*, in the pedestrian zone *Rua Zarco* with its cafés and bars and at the traditional-style stalls where grapes, melons and potatoes are on sale.

Things get very lively too in the new 2000-seater stadium for beach sports on the section of coast around *Penedo do Sono*, and on the new promenade lined with palm trees. Here on the landward side you can see the bold modern architecture of the market hall and the stone-and-glass *Centro do Artesanato*, an ensemble that accommodates the tourist information centre and craft shops, in some of which the craftspeople can be watched as they go about their work.

SIGHTSEEING

CASA DA CAMARA ANTIGA

The former town hall, flanked by two dragon trees, is a fine example of Portuguese Renaissance architecture. It was built in the 16th century, though several later alterations were made. The entrance, displaying the Portuguese coat of arms and the royal crown, is on the first floor, with two flights of steps leading up to it. Walk to the top of the steps to take a good look at the *Largo do Pelourinho*, which is shaded by palms and decoratively paved with stripes and a compass symbol in black and white.

CASA COLOMBO – MUSEU DO PORTO SANTO ★

The Columbus Museum collects exhibits about seafaring and the history of Porto Santo, and above all anything connected with the life and the deeds of the famous explorer: ships' models, marine charts, engraved portraits. The collection occupies two buildings. The one at the rear is considered to have been the house where Columbus lived. He is said to have spent some time here in about 1480 as a sugar trader. The locals like to tell that Christopher Columbus looked out to sea here while living in his father-in-law's house and hatched the first plans for his later crossing of the Atlantic Ocean. The museum informs its visitors not only about the background to Columbus and his voyages, but also about the age of the Spanish and Portuguese navigators in general. *Closed Mon | admission 1.50 euros | Travessa da Sacristia 2 and 4 | www.museucolombo-portosanto.com*

NOSSA SENHORA DA PIEDADE

An azulejo medallion shines as blue as the sea on the white façade of the parish church. This place of worship was founded in 1430 and attacked many

MARCO POLO HIGHLIGHTS

★ **Casa Colombo – Museu do Porto Santo**
The Museu do Porto Santo is a shrine to the navigator Christopher Columbus, who lived in this house for some time → p. 83

★ **Campo de Baixo**
A beach of fine sand runs all the way from the main town to the Ponta da Calheta, a distance of 5.6 mi → p. 84

times by pirates. In consequence the Morgada chapel on the south side is the only original part that remains. The church owes its Baroque appearance to various architects of the 17th century and houses an altar painting by Max Römer, a German painter who visited Porto Santo several times in the 1940s. *Rua Cristóvão Colombo*

FOOD & DRINK

O FORNO
The name tells diners what to expect: beef, fish and chicken prepared in the oven. Generous portions. *Rampa da Fontinha at the edge of Vila Baleira | tel. 2 91 98 51 41 | Budget–Moderate*

PÉ NA ÁGUA
Another eloquent name, and guests here really do almost have 'one foot in the water' when they enjoy the speciality of this beach restaurant: grilled squid. *Sítio das Pedras Pretas | tel. 2 91 98 31 14 | Moderate*

SALINAS
Good international food, right on the beach at the edge of town. The restaurant is part of the Torre Praia Hotel. *Rua Goulart Medeiros Praia da Fontinha | tel. 2 91 98 04 50 | Moderate*

SOLAR DO INFANTE
Modern surroundings for traditional cooking – lots of ingredients come from the sea. *Av. Dr. Manuel Gregório Pestana Jún. | in the Centro de Artesanato | tel. 2 91 98 52 70 | Moderate*

SHOPPING

CENTRO DE ARTESANATO
The shops in the craft centre sell miniature windmills, straw hats and various items made from sea shells. *Av. Dr. Manuel Gregório Pestana Jún.*

BEACHES

The golden-yellow sandy beach of ★ ● *Campo de Baixo* starts at the harbour

Not meals in a basket – the whole restaurant is a basket: Pé na Água

and goes all the way to *Ponta da Calheta (134 B 5) (₪ U 12)*. It is by far the most beautiful beach on the Madeira archipelago, and is the reason why Porto Santo has evolved into a tourist destination for holidaymakers from Madeira and mainland Portugal. In summer it is crowded with sun-hungry and sand-loving tourists. To the west of Vila Baleira it gets broader, and from there is supervised by lifeguards and equipped with toilets, showers (for a charge) and snack bars. To swim and sunbathe undisturbed, even in the peak season, go to the rocky INSIDERTIP bay of *Zimbralinho (134 B5) (₪ U 12)* with its turquoise water. This beach can only be reached by walking from the little pass near Morenos.

ACTIVITIES & SPORTS

In addition to windsurfing, kitesurfing, big-game fishing, sailing, rowing and canoeing (July to September only), you can try a Jeep safari and go paragliding. Book with an agency, e.g. *Lazermar (Rua João Gonçalves Zarco 66 | tel. 2 91 98 36 16) | www.lazermar.com.pt)*. On Penedo do Sono there is a go-kart circuit *(summer Sat/Sun 11am–2am)*.

GOLF
The 18-hole par-72 course *Porto Santo Golfe (green fee: 9 holes 40 euros, 18 holes 70 euros | Sítio da Lapeira de Dentro | tel. 2 91 98 37 77 and 2 91 98 37 78 | www.portosantogolfe.com)* is a round of almost 6.5 km (4 mi) with nine water obstacles. It was designed by Severiano Ballesteros, and a 9-hole course has been added. Golfers can use the facilities of a modest spa, and the clubhouse *restaurant (Moderate–Expensive)* is open to the public, serving good local and international cuisine.

Brilliant: a beach playground 9 km (5.6 mi) long

CYCLING
To explore the island, hire a bike from *Colombo | Av. Vieira de Castro 38 | tel. 2 91 98 44 38*.

HORSE RIDING
The INSIDERTIP *Centro Hípico (Sítio da Ponta | tel. 2 91 98 32 58)*, to which the *Restaurante Equestre (Budget–Moderate)* belongs, runs riding courses and hacks across the island.

DIVING
Dives and diving courses can be booked at the *Clube Naval de Porto Santo* and other diving bases. Porto Santo has an underwater attraction that Madeira lacks: a wreck, which can be explored on a dive *(Porto Santo Sub | at Porto Santo marina | tel. 2 91 98 32 59 | www.portosantosub.com)*.

WALKING

Three waymarked trails are shown on the map of the island that is handed out free of charge at the tourist office (e.g. the Vereda Pico Castelo and the Vereda Pico Branco/Terra Chá at the northeastern tip of the island).

PUB ZARCO

The island's legendary pub has loads of atmosphere and attracts quite a mix of people. *Daily from 6pm | Rua João Gonçalves Zarco*

Welcoming Vila Baleira in the evening: full of life in summer

ENTERTAINMENT

To the east of the historic centre of Vila Baleira the restaurants and bars of the *Penedo do Sono* entertainment quarter cater to the needs of visitors.

CHALLENGER

Hot beats into the early hours: mostly rock and pop, but hip-hop and other kinds of dance music too. *Summer only, daily from 10pm | Rua Estêvão Alencastre*

INSIDER TIP CINE CAFÉ

A popular retro-styled meeting place for a drink before hitting the clubs. *Rua Dr. Nuno Silvestre Teixeira (on the first floor, above the library of the cultural and congress centre)*

WHERE TO STAY

HOTEL PRAIA DOURADA

Centrally situated in Vila Baleira and only 200 m (220 yd) from the golden sandy beach of Praia Dourada. This three-star hotel has all the amenities that the average visitor to Porto Santo requires, from air-conditioned rooms to a wonderful outdoor pool. *100 rooms | Rua D. Estêvão de Alencastre | tel. 2 91 98 04 80 | www. portosantohotels.com/praia_dourada | Moderate*

HOTEL RESIDENCIAL CENTRAL

As the name suggests, this guesthouse has a very central location. The Porto do Abrigo and the beach are just a few minutes away. The rooms are simple and reasonably priced – something you don't often get on Porto Santo. *42 rooms | Rua Abel Magno Vasconcelos 1 | tel. 2 91 98 22 26 | Budget*

PARQUE DE CAMPISMO
A basic but extremely spacious campsite next to the Torre Praia hotel, with private access to the beach. *All year round | Fontinha | tel. 2 91 98 21 60*

PORTO SANTO
Contemporary design, a big garden and a sand hall where guests can benefit from the healing sand even in bad weather. Traditional touches such as basketwork furniture round off the attractions of this four-star hotel. *97 rooms | Campo de Baixo | tel. 2 91 98 01 40 | www.hotelportosanto.com | Expensive*

TORRE PRAIA
This comfortable, modern beach hotel close to the centre has a small pool, a large sun terrace and a tower bar. *66 rooms | Rua Goulart Medeiros | tel. 2 91 98 04 50 | www.torrepraia.pt | Expensive*

VILA BALEIRA THALASSA
Three-part complex of buildings. The part with the guest rooms is connected by a tunnel to the hydrotherapy centre and spa and to the beach club. Also on site: a pool for children and a playground. *256 rooms | Sítio do Cabeço da Ponta | tel. 2 91 98 08 00 | www.vilabaleira.com | Moderate–Expensive*

INFORMATION

POSTO DE TURISMO DO PORTO SANTO
Av. Dr. Manuel Gregório Pestana Júnior in the Centro de Artesanato | tel. 2 91 98 51 89 | www.ilhadourada.pt

DIRECÇAO REGIONAL DO AEROPORTO
Airport information. *tel. 2 91 98 01 20*

PORTO SANTO LINE
Ferries to and from Madeira can be booked online or through the hotels. *Tel. 2 91 21 03 00 | www.portosantoline.pt*

WHERE TO GO

CAMACHA (135 D 2) (*₥ V 10*)
This village (pop. 450) 4 km (2.5 mi) north of Vila Baleira is at the centre of most of the island's vineyards. Most of the grapes that ripen here are destined for the table, but some are pressed to make a number of different wines, which have a high alcohol content. If you want to taste a strong Porto Santo wine where it is made, try it under the thatched roof of the *Estrela do Norte* restaurant *(Sítio da Camacha | tel. 2 91 98 35 00 | Moderate)*. Near Camacha you can also stay in

LOW BUDGET

▶ The harbour of Porto Santo is a terminus not only for taxis and horse carriages, but also for *bus routes.*

▶ A few restaurants that lie outside the town offer their guests a *pick-up and drop-off service* from and to the hotel free of charge.

▶ The *Porto Santo Line* shipping company always has a special offer: e.g. a return ticket including an overnight stay that costs only 5–15 euros more than the price of the ticket only, depending on the season and time of sailing. *www.portosantoline.pt*

the quiet and charming *Quinta do Serrado (22 rooms | Sítio de Pedregal | tel. 2 91 98 02 70 | www.hotelquintadoserrado.com | Moderate)*. The estate has a small pool; in the restaurant delicious kid goat often features on the menu.

CAPELA DE NOSSA SENHORA DA GRAÇA
(135 D 3) *(Ɱ W 11)*

2 km (1.2 mi) northeast of Vila Baleira above *Casinhas* the little snow-white church of Nossa Senhora da Graça occupies the slope. An appearance of the Virgin in the 16th century was the reason for its construction. Destroyed in 1812, it was rebuilt in the early 1950s. Every year in mid-August the people of Porto Santo honour their patron saint with a procession.

FONTE DA AREIA (134 C 2) *(Ɱ V 10)*

6 km (3.7 mi) northwest of Vila Baleira fresh water springs from the ground with a backdrop of bizarrely shaped sandstone rock formations. With its pretty basin and lush green surroundings, the spring attracts locals and tourists who bring picnics. It used to be said that anyone who drank from the spring became 20 years younger. The water of the 'sand spring' was originally thought to have healing properties, and was later used as a public washing place.

PONTA DA CALHETA
(134 B 5) *(Ɱ U 12)*

6 km (3.7 mi) southwest of Vila Baleira, at the Ponta da Calheta, the end of Porto Santo is reached. However, directly off the southwestern tip of the island, looking almost close enough to touch, is the *Ilhéu de Baixo* with its strangely shaped limestone rocks. On some days a high jet of water spurts out of one of these rocks. The best place to enjoy this spectacle is the *O Calhetas* restaurant *(Ponta da Calheta | tel. 2 91 98 43 80 | Moderate)*, where fish specialities are brought to the table and a free transfer picks up guests from Vila Baleira and takes them back.

BOOKS & FILMS

▶ **Raquel's Daughters** – Helena Marques wrote this novel, a family saga set on 19th-century Madeira.

▶ **The Blandys of Madeira** – the history of 200 years of a family that shaped the island and its wine, by Marcus Binney.

▶ **The Gardens of Madeira** – expert descriptions of 30 gardens on the island by Gerald Luckhurst, lavishly illustrated

▶ **Moby Dick** – classic movie (1956) made by John Huston based on Herman Melville's novel, with Gregory Peck in the lead role. The opening sequences with whalers' boats were filmed on Madeira.

▶ **See you tomorrow, Mario** – documentary film by Solveig Nordlund about poor children on the streets of Madeira (1993)

▶ **Madeira – Pearl in the Atlantic** – impressions of some of the most beautiful parts of the island plus information (DVD, 2007)

Above Ponta da Calheta lies the ☀ vantage point called *Pico das Flores.* There is an unimpeded view from here across the entire southern part of the island. On the left are the summits of Cabeço do Zimbralinho, Cabeço do Dragoal and *Pico de Ana Ferreira (134 C 4) (ⓜ U 12)*, on the northern flank of which a beautiful INSIDER TIP formation of basalt columns can be seen. On its eastern side is the *Adega das Levadas (Rua Morenos | tel. 2 91 98 25 57 | Budget–Moderate)*, a good old-fashioned place to eat meat on the skewer with home-made bread and drink strong *vinho do Porto Santo* produced by the owners themselves.

The INSIDER TIP feast of São Pedro on 29 June is an impressive occasion. The patron saint of fishermen is honoured with Mass on the beach and a procession to his chapel at the foot of the Pico de Ana Ferreira.

PORTELA ☀ (135 D–E 3) (ⓜ W 11)

A strong breeze blows across Porto Santo on many days of the year. Centuries ago the inhabitants took advantage of this by building windmills to grind grain, which was then still plentiful on the island. The date of construction of the first mill is a matter of dispute. It is reported that there were 30 *moinhos* on the island in the early 20th century. By now most of them have become dilapidated, but three have been restored and placed on the Portela plateau.

QUINTA DAS PALMEIRAS
(134 C 3) (ⓜ V 11)

Industrious hands have created a manmade oasis in the desert: in the little botanical garden 5 km (3.1 mi) northwest of Vila Baleira, exotic birds flutter and twitter – flying free, in cages, and on perches. *Daily 10am–6pm | admission 2 euros | Sítio dos Linhares*

Elegant white calla lilies in Quinta das Palmeiras

SERRA DE FORA AND SERRA DE DENTRO

The ☀ lookout point at *Portela* is on the way to the karst landscape of Serra de Fora. On the edge of this sleepy village (135 E 3) (ⓜ W 11), 3 km (1.9 mi) northeast of Vila Baleira, a INSIDER TIP circular stone threshing floor *(aira)* can be made out. It is a reminder of the age of the navigators, when Porto Santo supplied grain to Portuguese ships on their voyages to Africa. 2 km (1.2 mi) to the north, Serra de Dentro (135 E 2) (ⓜ W 10) lies between the bare cones of the Pico Gandaia, Pico do Cabrito and Pico do Facho, the highest summit (517 m) on the island, from where beacon fires announced the approach of ships. This part of Porto Santo was once blessed with the most plentiful water supplies, but today nobody lives in the grey, partly decaying houses of basalt blocks any more.

TRIPS & TOURS

The tours are marked in green in the road atlas, pull-out map and on the back cover

1 PICO DO ARIEIRO/ PICO RUIVO – MADEI-RA'S HIGHEST MOUN-TAINS

★ This walk literally takes in the high points of Madeira, On all sides you will have a largely un-touched wilderness of jagged rocks and sparse mountain vegetation. However, this is a tough walk. You will need to ascend and descend heights of up to 700 m (765 yd) on paths that are steep in places with high steps in the rock. Here and there the route is narrow and eroded, and five unlit tunnels, often with flowing water, need to be traversed. Sure-footedness, a good head for heights and fitness are essential. Duration: ap-prox. 6,5 hours. Equipment: ankle-high walking boots, drinking water, food, binoculars, possibly also walking poles and a flashlight. To get to the start (and finish) take a hire car or a taxi to the car park at the Pico do Arieiro.

This tour is demanding but delightful in good weather. Set off as early as pos-sible in the morning from Madeira's third-highest mountain, the ☀ Pico do Arieiro. Walk past the highly controver-sial Nato radar installation and the new tourist centre with its souvenir shop, café and WC to ascend a few steps from the car park to the summit of the Arieiro. At the sight of the overwhelming mountain panorama you quickly forget the new buildings here. The view is at its most magical INSIDER TIP at sunrise when the weirdly shaped points of rock glow

Photo: Pico do Arieiro

Thrilling walking country – bizarre volcanic peaks, thundering waterfalls and a levada route with wonderful views of the coast

in the colours of mallows and lavender or when the setting sun bathes them in shades of copper, when the morning mist slowly parts to unveil the mountain peaks, white cushions of cloud sometimes settling around them.

As Madeira can often be hit by heavy storms and rainfall, with the risk of landslips in winter and forest fires in summer, the hiking trails are temporarily closed from time to time. In summer 2010, for example, forest fires destroyed parts of the vegetation in Madeira's high mountain terrain. Gradually the paths were repaired, and the plant life recovers quickly thanks to the wet winter climate. Do not walk along paths that have been closed: accidents and falls with potentially fatal consequences occur repeatedly because walkers ignore the barriers. An up-to-date list of which trails are open or closed is published at *www.provicmadeira.pt*. The route starts off as a wide path that is partly secured by fences. After almost 15 minutes you have already reached the rocky peak named **Ninho da Manta** (buzzard's nest) and the first lookout point, where you enjoy the view in the company of people who stroll here in sneakers. To get to the second *miradouro* you have to cross a narrow ridge, but the effort is rewarded by a view of the Pico Ruivo, which up to then is hidden behind the Pico das Torres (1851 m/2025 yd).

The route now makes a steep but secure lateral descent along the rock walls of the Pico do Cidrão (1798 m/1966 yd) across countless steps and through a gap in the rocks to the foot of the Pico do Gato (1780 m/1946 yd). Here, tree heath and gorse line the path, which soon disappears into the first tunnel and forks as you emerge. Choose whichever alternative looks in better condition as they merge again later. The left-hand path takes you through four more tunnels, the right-hand one past the eastern flank of the Pico das Torres.

After almost 2 hours what is now a single path, lined by tree heath, rises, gently at first and then in twists and turns. On the right a path branches off down to Achada do Teixeira, and straight ahead the route continues to the Pico Ruivo refuge hut, which is easy to spot. Keep left there until the trail forks, then take the path on the left (the one on the right leads to the Encumeada Pass after approx. 4.5 hours). Half an hour later you are already standing on the ☀️ Pico Ruivo (1862 m/2036 yd), Madeira's highest mountain, and the reward for your efforts is a magnificent 360° view (assuming the weather plays ball) taking in Paúl da Serra, the peaks around Curral das Freiras and the north coast of Madeira, and perhaps even extending as far as the island of Porto Santo and the Ponta de São Lourenço.

If you prefer not to return by the same way with energy-sapping ascents over rocky steps, the descent to Achada do

Teixeira takes less than an hour, but it is important to note that you need to have ordered a taxi to pick you up there, or you have to find a friendly driver who will give you a lift to Santana → p. 63.

2   BOCA DO RISCO – A VISTA OF THE NORTH COAST

Few walks on the island are as varied as this levada route from the eastern end of Madeira to Porto da Cruz: along the way you pass little clusters of houses, lonely pine forests, ravine-like gaps in the rock and cultivated terraces. There are overwhelming views at all times of the rugged north coast. The walk has a medium grade of difficulty, but you need to be sure of foot and have a good head for heights, as much of the path is exposed, i.e. drops away several hundred metres without any barrier. Moreover, heavy rains can wash away parts of the path, so you should only set out if the weather really is good. If you feel nervous about making the descent to the coast, then only walk as far as Boca do Risco and return to Machico from there (approx. 3 hours); otherwise the tour takes about 4,5 hours. Equipment: walking boots, food, drinking water, binoculars, perhaps walking poles. Getting there and away: bus no. 113 from Funchal or Machico to the Caniçal Tunnel (the stop is Pico do Facho), from Porto da Cruz bus no. 53 back to Machico. No. 113 runs on working days between 7am and 9am four times, on Saturdays three times, on Sundays twice. No. 53 runs four times after 1pm, on Saturdays only at 3.50pm and 5.25pm, on Sundays at 1.40pm.

Start from the little house on the left-hand side of the road at the western entrance to the old Caniçal Tunnel. The Levada do Caniçal starts just in front of it. First of all follow the concrete path, which soon becomes a narrow path over meadows. Straight ahead there is a beautiful ⋊⋉ view of the valley of Machico and the Pico do Facho, before you come to a little wood. Beyond it lies a wide-open scene of terraces planted with bananas, vines and vegetables.

Next you have to pass through a gap in

Continue in a westerly direction on a trail that at first has a dense cover of tree heath and shrubs. From here jungle-like greenery alternates with sections of sparse vegetation, and some exposed terrain has to be crossed. Soon the path approaches a wall of rock, becomes narrow and descends over loose gravel. You have passed a number of goat fences; at

Mountain walk with an eagle's view – Penha de Águia

the rocks, and then the levada goes right into a deep-cut little valley. Follow the watercourse until a path branches off right via two steps. This is the way to the Boca do Risco. It is stony but ascends gently, then drops into a valley again, goes through pine woods and once again between terraced fields. After about 1.5 hours and a slight turn to the left you have reached the rocky gap known as ⋊⋉ Boca do Risco. From an elevation of about 450 m (492 yd) you have a far-ranging view of the eastern part of the steep, largely unspoiled north coast.

the ⋊⋉ sixth fence pause to enjoy the view of the Eagle Rock (Penha de Águia) and neighbouring Porto da Cruz.

You have now managed more than half of the route, and the landscape starts to change character once again, presenting slopes of eucalyptus and pine. A few stone steps take you down to a deep cleft with a watercourse and through two similar little canyons. Shortly after this you will see an unsurfaced road, which leads at the same elevation to a gap and then left into a valley of terraced fields. However, you are still on a mountain ridge parallel to the coast, alongside a water-course. The first houses now appear, and from here the road is asphalted. Follow it steeply downhill for almost 1000 m until you almost reach a rise. Here a concrete path branches off sharply to the right, and on the left steps go down from this path to a clearly visible levada path. Follow this past fields of vegetables, cross an unsurfaced road and turn left towards the sea when you come to an animal shelter built into the rock.

The route now leads over a little ridge and steeply downhill once again, through a stream bed which is dry in summer and across the slope to a group of houses. Above them you will encounter steps; descend here. Next keep left over the hill until you reach a paved track. A wall of stone shows where you branch off to the right towards the coast. You still have to negotiate a stream bed with a collapsed bridge, and then the trail continues straight ahead, climbs briefly once more, and shortly after that you ascend a few stone steps to reach the road that takes you west in the direction of the Eagle Rock. Less than 1000 m further on you have arrived at the main square of **Porto da Cruz** → p. 65.

3 RABAÇAL – PURE WATER AND UNTOUCHED NATURE

Almost everyone who goes walking on Madeira comes to Rabaçal. In this wet valley between the Paúl da Serra plateau and the mountain range from Pico da Fajã da Lenha to Fanal that points to the north coast, there are many places within a small area where you feel as if you have entered a jungle. Here dense greenery borders the levadas and streams, and spring water cascades over walls of rock. This walk has an easy to medium level of difficulty.

Getting there and away: a hire car or taxi to the car park up on the ER 110 near Rabaçal. Local companies run day trips. The paths can be slippery because the valley basin is very wet. **Equipment:** stout shoes with soles that grip well, possibly protection against rain and some food. **Duration:** 40 minutes or about 2 hours.

Cascata do Risco and **25 Fontes** are the two most attractive and popular destinations from Rabaçal. The starting point is always the walkers' car park at Rabaçal on the road from Paúl da Serra. Here you walk downhill for 40 minutes along a track that has been asphalted but is closed to cars to the forest lodge of Rabaçal, where there are picnic spots, toilets and a small state-run hostel for walkers who have booked in advance. There are signposts to show you the way to the various trails. Take the broad, level path to **Levada do Risco** and follow it to where the signposted way to '25 Fontes'

branches off. Now you have to decide whether to see the waterfall sooner or later.

If you take the first option, walk straight ahead by the levada. After about 15 minutes a fenced path forks off to the right to the basin of the Risco waterfall and ends at a ☆ viewing terrace. Here you can marvel at the veil of droplets covering the rock face. Return the way you came. It's not advisable to walk under the cascade and through the tunnel, as this path has been blocked for safety reasons after just a few metres.

For the walk to the 25 Springs follow the sign pointing left at the place where the turn-off to Risco goes right. Stone steps, hairpins and a second set of steps take you to the **Levada das 25 Fontes**, which you follow against the direction of the flow. It's not far to a ☆ viewpoint on the right from which you can make out the further course of the levada and look down into the valley.

At the place where the levada disappears into the mountain, stone steps with a wooden balustrade show the way to a bridge, which you cross and climb again to the levada. A little further on from here you can **INSIDER TIP** look down into the Risco valley. Following the levada wall cross the slope, which is secured only by tree heath as far as a plateau, then take a right curve into the valley of the 25 Springs. Here the path goes straight on and descends to the Levada da Rocha Vermelha, but instead you should stay with the water channel until you reach a second bridge, where you turn to the right with the wider levada. After a few minutes the valley bottom opens out, and you have reached the 25 Springs. In the dry summer months only a little water dribbles over the rocks, but at other times you can hope to see lots of it splashing down from the springs. Return by the same route, past the forest lodge and then back up to the car park.

25 Fontes: thirsty walkers gather to drink from the springs

SPORTS &
ACTIVITIES

With its levadas and mountain paths Madeira is a varied paradise for walkers. Golfers enjoy a round on courses in spectacular scenery. And there is a wide range of water sports too.

New activities aimed at younger visitors are on the up. The range of outdoor pursuits now encompasses trekking, canyoning, sea kayaking, quad-bike tours, hang- and paragliding, climbing, mountainbiking and Jeep safaris. The island government has also made major investments in coast and beach tourism. On the north, east and south coasts new water parks and marinas have been built. Existing access to beaches (for example at Reis Magos) has been improved, in other places completely new infrastructure has been created (as in Machico, Porto da Cruz, São Vicente, São Jorge, Ponta Delgada and Ribeira do Faial). The beach at Garajau can now be reached by cable car; Lugar de Baixo now boasts a beach of golden sand to compete with the bay at Calheta.

BIG GAME FISHING

Ocean fishing trips can be booked through various local agencies, at hotel reception or direct from the marina in Funchal. Information: *Katherine B' Big Game Fishing (tel. 2 91 75 26 85 | mobile tel. 9 17 59 99 90 | www.fishmadeira.com); Turipesca (tel. 2 91 23 10 63 | www.madeirafishingcentre.com); Nautisantos Big Game Fishing (tel. 2 91 23 13 12 | www.*

**From mountain biking to putting –
all sorts of new activities complement the
classic pastimes of walking and water sports**

nautisantosfishing.com). All boats oper-
ate from the marina in Funchal.

CANYONING

Advanced-level hiking: with a wetsuit,
helmet and safety ropes participants
descend through canyons and over
waterfalls. This adventure gives you a
real adrenalin rush – and is a whole
lot of fun. Various operators organise
canyoning, e.g. *Ventura do Mar | Mari-
na do Funchal | tel. 2 9128 00 33 | www.*

*venturadomar.com/trek.htm | 60 euros
per person.*

DIVING

Exotic-looking species of fish abound in
the crystal-clear waters and delight di-
vers as much as the bizarre underwater
lava formations and caves. The diving
stations are on the south and southeast
coasts as well as on Porto Santo. The
greatest diversity of sea life can be seen
in the ☺ ● *Garajau marine national*

park, which was established in 1986 to protect marine creatures. For information see e.g.: *Atalaia Diving Center (in the Hotel Rocamar | Caniço de Baixo | tel. 2 91 93 43 30 | www.atalaia-madeira.com); Madeira Divepoint (in the Hotel Carlton | Largo António Nobre | Funchal | tel. 2 91 23 95 79 | www.madeiradivepoint.com).*

GOLF

The sites of Madeira's greens have been chosen for their beauty. From the 27-hole course of ❄️ *Santo da Serra (tel. 2 91 55 01 00 | www.santodaserra golf.com)* players have a breathtaking INSIDER TIP view of the east coast. In the hilly country east of Funchal the 18-hole course at ❄️ *Palheiro Golf (Rua do Balancal 29 | Funchal | tel. 2 91 79 01 20 | www.palheirogolf.com)* also has impressive scenery. A Nick Faldo course opens for business in 2012 in Ponta do Pargo. This 18-hole course designed by the three-time Masters champion is spectacularly located above the cliffs of the west coast.

HANGGLIDING & PARAGLIDING

The topography of Madeira is a genuine challenge for paragliders and hang gliders, because there are not many places to take off, and even fewer to land. Beginners can try a tandem flight. Contact: *International Paragliding Center | Rua Achada de Santo Antão 199 | Arco da Calheta | mobile tel. 9 64 13 39 07 | www.madeira-paragliding.com*

MOUNTAIN BIKING

Steep climbs, breakneck descents, lonely mountain and forest tracks – what more could a biker want? There is a bike park in Porto Moniz and no shortage of hire shops near tourist hotels, e.g. *Bike Zone | | Forum Madeira | Estrada Monumental | Funchal*

SAILING & BOAT TRIPS

A sailing licence allows you to hire a dinghy from *Aquasports* in the Lido pool complex *(Funchal | Rua do Gorgulho)*. You can also book a trip on a chartered luxury yacht or in a group on a smaller boat – to cross to the Ilhas Desertas, for example. Some trips include the opportunity to watch whales and dolphins. *Bonita da Madeira (moors in Funchal marina | tel. 2 91 76 22 18 | www.bonita-da-madeira.com)*: this two-masted ship – a 20-metre wooden caravel built in 1996 – can accommodate up to 50 passengers for whale- and dolphin-watching trips on Wednesdays and Sundays, for a INSIDER TIP trip to the Ilhas Desertas on Tuesdays, Thursdays and Saturdays, and for a tour of Madeira's loveliest bays on Fridays. *Lobosonda (Calheta marina | mobile tel. 9 68 40 09 80 | www.lobosonda.com):* the *Ribeira Brava*, a lovingly restored 1960s fishing boat, approaches whales and dolphins gently without disturbing them as passengers learn all about these marine creatures. *Ventura do Mar (Funchal marina) | tel. 2 91 28 00 33 | www.venturadomar.com)*: a 16-metre two-masted sailing boat built in 1963 specialises in trips to observe sea birds. It goes out to Cabo Girão, the Ilhas Desertas and on sunset tours.

SURFING & WINDSURFING

The waves of the coasts of Madeira are a real challenge for surfers and windsurfers. The waters at Jardim do Mar and Paúl do Mar, above all, as well as those east of São Vicente provide excellent conditions for these sports. The best time of year is September to February. See *www.*

nels all year round, and others are unlit. More and more walking trails are being equipped with waymarkers, fences and hand-ropes, so that some walks which once presented the dan-

Indispensable if you want to see unforgettable views on Madeira: stout shoes

surf-forecast.com to check out the surf at different spots.

WALKING

The best way to really get to know the landscape of Madeira is on foot – e.g. by doing a levada or mountain walk. Take care when planning a tour and bear in mind that the weather can change quickly, with fog and rain appearing or temperatures dropping suddenly. There is water in some tun-

ger of a fall are now safe. As the start and finish of a walk may be far apart, it is often useful to agree a pick-up with a taxi driver in order to get back to base.

Many companies and individuals offer organised walks, and their brochures and contact details can be found in the hotels, e.g. *Madeira Explorers (Centro Comercial Monumental Lido | tel. 2 91 76 37 01 | mobile tel. 9 69 52 80 22 | www.madeira-levada-walks.com)*.

TRAVEL WITH KIDS

Only a few years ago parents needed plenty of imagination to keep their kids happy when taking a holiday on Madeira. Nowadays there is a much bigger range of attractions for the young generation.

The coasts may fall steeply into the Atlantic, and the sea may often be rough, but man-made beach lagoons that slope gently into the water have now been created, for example in Calheta and Machico. And the lava pools at Porto Moniz are an exciting alternative to beaches.

FUNCHAL

In Funchal the family favourites are the *Barreirinha pool*, and especially two places to swim on the coastal promenade in the hotel zone: the *Lido* and the *Ponta Gorda pool*.

The promenade is also the site of *Madeira Magic*, where children can learn about gravity, optical illusions and the inside of the human body in a playful and interactive way. *Tue–Sun 10am–6pm | admission 5 euros, children (age 3–17) 4 euros | Rua Ponta da Cruz 25 (130 B 6) (⊕ K 8) | www.madeira-magic.com*

Kids' eyes light up at the sight of the ● *Santa Maria*. This replica of one of Co-

lumbus's ships anchors in the harbour (130 B–C 6) (⊕ L 8); for trips to Cabo Girão and back the crew dress as pirates, and with a little luck leaping dolphins will escort the ship. *Daily 10.30am and 3pm | trip lasts approx. 3 hours | 30 euros, children 15 euros | tel. 2 91 22 03 27 and 2 91 22 56 95 | www.madeirapirateboat.com*

Kids can discover the secrets of electricity at the INSIDER TIP ▶ *Museu da Electricidade,* which was once Funchal's power station for district heating. They can even generate electricity themselves! *Tue–Sat 10am–12.30pm and 2pm–6pm | admission 2 euros | Rua da Casa da Luz 2 (130 C 6) (⊕ L 8)*

THE SOUTH

Calheta holds several treats in store for young holidaymakers: building sandcastles on the beach or visiting the old *sugar-cane mill (127 D 2) (⊕ C–D 5–6) (Engenho da Calheta | Mon–Fri 8am–6pm, Sat/Sun 9am–1pm and 2–6pm | free admission)*, where all sorts of antique-looking machinery is on display. If you want to take kids on an expedition into Madeira's mountains, a stop on the way at the *Quinta Pedagógica dos Prazeres (120 C 6) (⊕ B–C 4–5)* is a chance to

Nature is an adventure – explore old ships, see colourful fish and discover secrets

see ostriches and llamas. Many breeds of hens, pigs, horses and donkeys can also be seen in the quinta garden. *Daily 9am–8pm, in summer till 9pm | admission to the garden free, zoo 1 euro*

On the Paúl da Serra (122 A 6) *(Ⓜ E–F 4)* plateau the *Jungle Rain* café restaurant *makes for an entertaining break*. Jungle stage sets and dummy animals create a wonderful rainforest atmosphere. *Sítio do Ovil | tel. 2 91 82 01 50 | Moderate*

THE NORTH

There's lots to discover and plenty of ways to work off energy on climbing frames and other playground equipment for kids in the *Parque Temático da Madeira* in Santana (125 D 4) *(Ⓜ M 3)*. *Daily 10am–7pm (closed Mon in the off-season) | admission 10 euros, children 8 euros | Fonte da Pedra | www.parquete maticodamadeira.pt*

In the reconstructed *fort in Porto Moniz* (121 D 1) *(Ⓜ C–D 1)* the sharks and many other creatures of the deep are sure to

delight young and old at the *Aquário da Madeira*. *Daily 9am–6pm | admission 7 euros, children 4 euros | Rua Forte São João Batista | www.aquariodamadeira. com*

THE EAST

The *Praia das Palmeiras* in Santa Cruz (132 A 5) *(Ⓜ O 7)* caters for kids with its seawater pools, floating islands and comic figures. There are also plastic toys free of charge, a treasure island with a 'real' dragon and a climbing area. *Daily 9am–7pm*

A little further inland in Ribeira da Boaventura (132 A 4) *(Ⓜ O 7)* INSIDER TIP *Aquaparque*, which was built to hold several thousand visitors, has fun pools, five water chutes and an artificial stream that meanders around the swimming pools. *Daily 10am–6pm | admission 6.50 euros, children aged 5–12 4 euros | www.aqua parque.com*

FESTIVALS & EVENTS

The sound of fireworks going off in the morning announces imminent events: grape picking, cherry harvest, spring blossom – for all of these a *festa* is held on the island. Religious festivals are marked by lengthy celebration of Mass and processions; after that things get a whole lot more worldly with folklore, disco music, dancing and a hearty meal. As well as the traditional festivities, there is room in the calendar for newer events such as the International Film Festival in Funchal *(Festival Internacional de Cinema do Funchal)*, which has been held each year since 2006 , or the *Fins de Semana Musicais*, weekends when classical music is performed in the gardens and concert halls of Funchal (July/August).

PUBLIC HOLIDAYS

1 Jan. *Ano Novo* (New Year), **Sexta-feira Santa** (Good Friday), **25 April** *Dia de Portugal* (Anniversary of the Carnation Revolution), **1 May** *Dia do Trabalho* (Labour Day), **Corpo de Deus** (Corpus Christi), **10 June** *Dia de Camões* (anniversary of the death of the national poet Luís Vaz de Camões), **15 Aug.** *Assunção* (Assumption of the Virgin), **5 Oct.** *Dia da República* (Day of the Republic), *1 November Todos os Santos* (All Saints

Day), **1 Dec.** *Dia da Restauração* (Independence Day), **8 Dec.** *Imaculada Conceição* (Immaculate Conception), **25 Dec.** *Natal* (Christmas)

FESTIVALS & EVENTS

FEBRUARY

▶ *Carnival:* big parade from Avenida do Infante to the centre of Funchal in the style of Rio de Janeiro with samba dance groups and floats

APRIL/MAY

▶ ★ *Festa da Flor:* flower festival for the spring blossom in Funchal. The highlight is a procession through the streets of floats decorated with flowers *(two weeks after Easter)*

JUNE

▶ *Festival do Atlântico:* high-calibre concerts and touring ballet troupes in Funchal and Calheta, combined with an international firework competition and street music *(all month, firework concerts each Saturday)*

▶ INSIDER TIP *Altares de São João:* saint's day festival with an altar-building competition and lots to eat around Praça do Carmo in Funchal *(week of 24 June)*

Floral displays and fireworks – the Madeirans love to celebrate, and find plentiful occasions to do so all year round

JULY

▶ *48 horas a Bailar:* folklore festival in Santana with performances of dance and music, information stands run by local communities, home-made specialities and fair

▶ *Feira do Porto Moniz:* big agricultural fair on a forested area above this coastal town

AUGUST

▶ *Nossa Senhora do Monte:* religious highlight of the year. On the day of the Assumption of the Virgin the people of Madeira honour the patron of their island with a pilgrimage. The faithful come from far and wide to the lavishly decorated church of Monte

SEPTEMBER

▶ *Madeira Wine Festival:* wine tasting and exhibitions on Avenida Arriaga in Funchal and in Estreito de Câmara de Lobos

▶ *Festa da Nossa Senhora da Piedade:* procession of boats in Caniçal, at which a statue of the Virgin is conveyed by sea

▶ *Festa do Pêro:* apple festival in Ponta do Pargo with a tractors parade and sale of farmers' products and home-made jam

▶ *Festival Colombo:* over three days Porto Santo pays tribute to its most famous inhabitant with a medieval market, street performers and a historical parade. The climax is a re-enactment of Columbus' departure on the quay at Vila Baleira.

OCTOBER/NOVEMBER/DECEMBER

▶ *Festa do Senhor dos Milagres:* night-time procession in honour of a miracle-working image of Jesus in Machico *(9 Oct)*

▶ *Chestnut Festival* in Curral das Freiras with chestnut bread and liqueur, and folklore *(1 Nov)*

▶ *Festas do Fim do Ano:* the end of the old year begins in late November in Funchal. The climax of the celebrations is New Year's Eve, when the famous ★ New Year fireworks are set off in the bay and all around the slopes of this great natural amphitheatre.

NOTES

MARCO POLO TRAVEL GUIDES

ALGARVE
AMSTERDAM
ANDALUCÍA
ATHENS
AUSTRALIA
AUSTRIA
BALI
  LOMBOK,
  GILI ISLANDS
BANGKOK
BARCELONA
BERLIN
BRAZIL
BRUGES, GHENT &
  ANTWERP
BRUSSELS
BUDAPEST
BULGARIA
CALIFORNIA
CAMBODIA
CANADA EAST
CANADA WEST
  ROCKIES
CAPE TOWN
  WINE LANDS,
  GARDEN ROUTE
CAPE VERDE
CHANNEL ISLANDS
CHICAGO
  & THE LAKES
CHINA
COLOGNE
COPENHAGEN
CORFU
COSTA BLANCA
  VALENCIA
COSTA BRAVA
  BARCELONA
COSTA DEL SOL
  GRANADA
CRETE
CUBA
CYPRUS
  NORTH AND
  SOUTH
DRESDEN
DUBAI
DUBLIN
DUBROVNIK &
  DALMATIAN COAST

EDINBURGH
EGYPT
EGYPT'S RED
  SEA RESORTS
FINLAND
FLORENCE
FLORIDA
FRENCH ATLANTIC
  COAST
FRENCH RIVIERA
  NICE, CANNES &
  MONACO
FUERTEVENTURA
GRAN CANARIA
GREECE
HAMBURG
HONG KONG
  MACAU
ICELAND
INDIA
INDIA SOUTH
  GOA & KERALA
IRELAND
ISRAEL
ISTANBUL
ITALY
JORDAN
KOS
KRAKOW
LAKE GARDA

LANZAROTE
LAS VEGAS
LISBON
LONDON
LOS ANGELES
MADEIRA
  PORTO SANTO
MADRID
MALLORCA
MALTA
  GOZO
MAURITIUS
MENORCA
MILAN
MONTENEGRO
MOROCCO
MUNICH
NAPLES &
  THE AMALFI COAST
NEW YORK
NEW ZEALAND
NORWAY
OSLO
PARIS
PHUKET
PORTUGAL
PRAGUE

RHODES
ROME
SAN FRANCISCO
SARDINIA
SCOTLAND
SEYCHELLES
SHANGHAI
SICILY
SINGAPORE
SOUTH AFRICA
SRI LANKA
STOCKHOLM
SWITZERLAND
TENERIFE
THAILAND
TURKEY
TURKEY
  SOUTH COAST
TUSCANY
UNITED ARAB
  EMIRATES
USA SOUTHWEST
VENICE
VIENNA
VIETNAM
ZÁKYNTHOS

- PACKED WITH INSIDER TIPS
- BEST WALKS AND TOURS
- FULL-COLOUR PULL-OUT MAP
  AND STREET ATLAS

LINKS, BLOGS, APPS & MORE

LINKS

▶ www.madeiratourism.com This is the official tourism website of Madeira, with pages in English. It gives a good overview of what to do and where to stay

▶ www.madeiraarchipelago.com An independent database with photos, films and a variety of information about the island. Madeira is presented not only as a holiday paradise but also as the home of the photographers, most of them locals

▶ www.madeira-web.com More information for your holiday, including weather, walks and pictures live from various webcams

▶ www.madeira-island.com This site is useful for shopping, museums and details of the festivals celebrated on the island

BLOGS & FORUMS

▶ http://blog.madeirawindbirds.com English-language blog of a travel operator in Funchal that is specialised in sustainable nature tourism (e.g. bird watching, whale watching). Also deals with up-to-date green topics

▶ http://madeiraislanddirect.com/blog Full English-language blog about current events. News, information and lots of themes are presented concisely and illustrated with matching photos or films. Sponsored by a real-estate company

▶ www.madeirablog.eu Private blog with lots of amusing photos and helpful information

▶ www.netmadeira.com/webcams-madeira The most pressing question on Madeira is: what's the weather like? The webcams are a godsend for walkers

Regardless of whether you are still preparing your trip or already on Madeira: these addresses will provide you with more information, videos and networks to make your holiday even more enjoyable.

who are planning a hiking tour on the other side of the island

▶ www.vimeo.com/13538576 Some good photos, and above all fantastic films of flying over the hills of Madeira taken using the ‚flycam' of the Paragliding Centre in Arco da Calheta

▶ www.youtube.com/watch?v=PGKP8EsP2Nk A slide show of historic photographs. If you make a direct comparison of the scene today with these 100-year-old pictures, in some places it seems as if time has stood still

▶ www.youtube.com/watch?v=oETGAkOtSIU Even if you are not a diver, you can get a magic view of the world of fish, monk seals, octopuses and rays of the coast of Madeira by watching the film 'Madeira Aquatica' taken by the underwater photographer Gonçalo Gomes

▶ madeira-street-map Apple provides this detailed street and road map of the island and the capital Funchal for downloads for your iPhone

▶ appbrain For Android phones appbrain has detailed street mapping of the island of flowers

▶ http://secure.hospitalityclub.org/hc/hcworld.php?region=1907 This is the best source for finding low-cost accommodation on Madeira and at the same time getting to know the locals. Registered individual travellers will find welcoming friends via the Hospitality Club

▶ www.facebook.com/SecretMadeira This Facebook community (in Portuguese, sometimes also in English) plans activities and events. Tips like secret places to swim complete with tempting pictures have been known to appear here.

TRAVEL TIPS

ACCOMMODATION

There are currently about 31,000 beds for visitors to Madeira, mostly in Funchal and Caniço, and the majority are four- or five-star hotels (graded by Portuguese standards). Add to this apartment hotels ranging from basic to luxurious, *estalagens* (simple hotels), *albergarias*, guesthouses *(pensão, residencial)* and rural accommodation organised by the *turismo de habitação (TH)* or *turismo rural (TR)*. Some of these were once residences of the wealthy *(quintas)* – though hotels too like to use this coveted name. For information on accommodation see e.g. *www.madeirarural.com* and *www. madeira-web.com*

ARRIVAL

✈ Package holidays with a flight and accommodation are the simplest and generally also the cheapest way to go. A charter flight from western europe in summer without hotel costs 300–400 euros. The prices are similar for TAP Portugal's scheduled flights, which go several times daily – but you have to change in Lisbon. In summer TAP also flies several times a week from Lisbon direct to Porto Santo. Otherwise you can get there from Madeira up to five times daily with SATA flights (flying time approx. 20 minutes). Madeira's *airport (tel. 2 9152 07 00)* is located in Santa Catarina near Santa Cruz, some 12.4 mi from the centre of Funchal. Bus routes 20, 53, 78, 113, 208 connect it with the city (the bus stop is 100 m to the right of the arrivals concourse) and the Aerobus, which stops directly in front of arrivals, runs to the hotel zone in Funchal.

🚢 Cruise ships often put in at Funchal. The Spanish shipping line Armas operates a once-weekly car ferry from Tenerife via Funchal to Portimão (Algarve) and back *(www.navieraarmas.com)*. The Lobo Marinho ferry crosses daily from Funchal to Madeira's sister island Porto Santo *(approx. 2 hours / return ticket from 42.10 euros at off-peak times / tel. 2 9121 03 00 / www.portosantoline.pt).*

RESPONSIBLE TRAVEL

It doesn't take a lot to be environmentally friendly whilst travelling. Don't just think about your carbon footprint whilst flying to and from your holiday destination but also about how you can protect nature and culture abroad. As a tourist it is especially important to respect nature, look out for local products, cycle instead of driving, save water and much more. If you would like to find out more about eco-tourism please visit: *www.ecotourism.org*

CAMPING

Camping on Madeira other than on official campsites is allowed only with a permit issued by the forestry authorities *(Direcção Regional de Florestas / tel. 2 9174 00 60 / www.sra.pt/drf)*. In this case the local forest offices direct campers to the sites that they authorise. Madeira's campsite is close to Ribeira da Janela, and on Porto Santo there is an area for tents near the main town Vila Baleira.

From arrival to weather

CAR HIRE

National and international car hire firms have offices at Madeira and Porto Santo airports, as well as in Funchal and Vila Baleira. Local operators tempt visitors with special offers, but it is certainly worth comparing their prices with the offers available when booking at home. Drivers of hire cars must be at least 21 years old. A car costs between 30 and 70 euros per day, with unlimited mileage. 13 per cent tax is usually added to these prices. Delivery of the vehicle to a hotel in Funchal is usually free of charge, but an extra fee (approx. 15 euros) is payable if delivery to and collection from the airport is necessary.

CLIMATE

Madeira enjoys a mild climate all year round. Even in January and February it is exceptional for the daytime temperature on the south coast to fall below 15 °C. The warmest months are July, August and September, but even then the thermometer rarely shows more than 25 °C. Go prepared for rain showers, especially in winter and spring.

The weather on Madeira can be extremely changeable, and differ from one place to another at any one time. The weather forecasts pinned to hotel notice boards (e.g. from www.madeira-weather.info) should only be seen as a general guide. Webcams (e.g. www.madeirawebcams.com) may be more helpful. When the trade winds blow from the northeast, it is often cloudy in the mountains and on the north coast, but stable. A southeast wind (leste) from the Sahara means warm and sunny weather for most of the island. West winds cause changeable and rainy weather, as they carry alternating fronts of warm and cold air.

BUDGETING

Poncha	2–3 euros	
	for a rum cocktail	
Bica	70 Cent	
	for an espresso coffee	
Lapas	6–8 euros	
	for a portion of limpets	
Petrol	1,30 euros	
	for 1 l of unleaded	
Pool	1–3 euros	
	per day at sea-water pools	
Souvenir	18–25 euros	
	for a bottle of Madeira wine (aged for 10 years)	

CONSULATES

– British honorary consulate | Mon, Tue, Thu, Fri 10am–12.30pm | Rua da Alfandega 10, 3C | Funchal | tel. 2 91 21 28 60 | e-mail: Britcon.Funchal@NetMadeira.com
– U.S. consular agency | Mon–Fri 9am–1pm | Rua da Alfandega 10, 2F | Funchal | tel. 2 91 123 56 26 | e-mail: ACAFunchal@eua.website.pt

CUSTOMS

Within the European Union goods for personal use can be imported and exported duty-free. However note that some limits should not be exceeded, e.g. 800 cigarettes, 10 litres of spirits per person (over the age of 17). Visitors from other countries must observe the following limits, except for items for personal use. Duty free are: max. 50 g perfume, 200 cigarettes, 50 cigars, 250 g tobacco, 1 L of spirits (over 22% vol.), 2 L of spirits (under 22% vol.), 2 L of any wine.

DRIVING

The speed limit on Madeira in towns is 50 km/h (30 mph), on country roads 90 km/h (55 mph) and on the *via rápida*, Madeira's fast highway, 100 km/h (62 mph). In case of a breakdown drivers leaving the vehicle must wear a high-viz jacket. The main roads on Madeira and Porto Santo are surfaced with asphalt and good condition; many of them now run through tunnels. Parking spaces in the centre of Funchal are scarce and cost money.

ELECTRICITY

The two-pin sockets in Portugal and on Madeira are the same as those in continental Europe, so visitors from Britain and North America should take an adapter. The power supply is 220 volts AC.

EMERGENCY SERVICES

– Emergency/ambulance: *tel. 112*
– SANAS sea rescue: *tel. 2 91 23 01 12*
– Mountain rescue (Protecção Civil): *tel. 2 91 70 01 12*
– Breakdown service: *tel. 8 00 29 02 90*

HEALTH

Many hotels can call a hotel doctor. A medical consultation should be paid for immediately. EU citizens can recoup the costs at home by producing an invoice. It is recommended to take out a holiday health insurance policy, as some costs for medicine and treatment have to be borne by the patient, and in some cases return transport to the home country may be necessary. The EHIC (European Health Insurance Card) entitles EU citizens to treatment in state hospitals and health centres, e.g. in the *Centro de Saúde* in Funchal *(Mon–Fri 8am–8pm | Rua das Hortas 67 | tel. 2 91 20 87 00)*. The state-run *Hospital Cruz de Carvalho (Av. Luís de Camões | tel. 2 91 70 56 00)* is close to the hotel zone in Funchal. The small private *Clínica da Sé (Rua das Murças 42 | tel. 2 91 20 76 76)*, where English is spoken, provides specialist help from consultants round the clock. English-speaking dentists are also available here. All towns on the island have a health clinic *(centro de saúde)*. The address on Porto Santo is *Centro de Saúde Porto Santo (Rua Dr. José Diamantino Lima | tel. 2 91 98 00 60)*. There are enough pharmacies, at least in the towns *(farmácias, postos de medicamentos)*, and one of them is always open; the up-to-date schedule of opening times is on display in the window of every pharmacy.

IMMIGRATION

EU citizens need only an ID card or passport. Children under the age of 16 must be registered on a parent's passport or carry a child's passport. A valid passport is required for entry into Portugal (Non-EU). All children must travel with their own passport.

INFORMATION

TOURISM ORGANISATION
TURISMO DE PORTUGAL
info@visitportugal.com | www.visitportugal.com
DIRECÇÃO REGIONAL DO TURISMO
Tel. 2 91 21 19 00 | www.turismomadeira.pt
– Tourist information in Funchal:
Av. Arriaga 16 | tel. 2 91 21 19 02
– Tourist information at the airport:
arrivals hall | tel. 2 91 52 49 33

CÂMARA MUNICIPAL DE PORTO SANTO
Rua Dr. Nuno Silvestre Teixeira (Edifício de Serviços Públicos) | tel. 2 91 98 06 40 | www.cm-portosanto.pt

LANGUAGE

The people of Madeira speak Portuguese with their own dialect, which the mainland Portuguese recognise at once. Visitors to the island can get by very well speaking English. In hotels, restaurants and agencies the staff have often been well trained at the school of tourism to look after foreign visitors and may be fluent in more than one foreign language. Spanish is understood quite well on Madeira, but speaking Spanish to the locals is not the way to make yourself popular. Portuguese is, spoken worldwide by approx. 210 million people, and anyone who would like to learn it on Madeira can book an individual language course (contact tourist office for information).

MEDIA

TV channels in English are available in many hotels. International newspapers are on sale at kiosks, often a day after publication, and the English-speaking magazine Madeira Life has lots of information, including bus timetables and events listings.

MONEY & PRICES

As in the rest of Portugal, the currency in circulation on Madeira is the euro. Even in rural areas cash machines (ATMs, multibancos) can now be found almost everywhere. The amount that can be withdrawn is limited to 200 euros, i.e. if you need 400 euros you need to withdraw cash twice and pay the bank charge both times. Payment by credit card or EC cheque card is accepted in larger hotels and most restaurants and shops that do business with tourists. Price levels are not much different from those in other EU countries. Basic foodstuffs such as bread are cheap thanks to state subsidies, but products such as cosmetics and toiletries tend to be expensive. The cost of living is lower outside the main tourist areas.

OPENING HOURS

Tourist offices, small shops and public institutions such as museums are normally open Mon–Fri 9am–12.30pm and 2.30–6pm, Sat 9am–1pm. Banks open Mon–Fri 9am–3pm. Supermarkets and shopping centres are open daily as a rule

CURRENCY CONVERTER

£	€	€	£
1	1.10	1	0.90
3	3.30	3	2.70
5	5.50	5	4.50
13	14.30	13	11.70
40	44	40	36
75	82.50	75	67.50
120	132	120	108
250	275	250	225
500	550	500	450

$	€	€	$
1	0.70	1	1.40
3	2.10	3	4.20
5	3.50	5	7
13	9.10	13	18.20
40	28	40	56
75	52.50	75	105
120	84	120	168
250	175	250	350
500	350	500	700

For current exchange rates see www.xe.com

until 10pm without a midday break. Unless otherwise shown, the restaurants described in this guide are open daily noon–3pm and from 6pm (usually until approx. 11pm). Evening shopping is possible in shopping centres (e.g. *Madeira Shopping* and *Forum Madeira*) until 11pm and at the weekend even until midnight.

PHONE & MOBILE PHONE

The cheapest option for an overseas call is to go to the main post office. In Funchal and other towns there are coin-operated and card-operated phones from which calls overseas *(internacionais)* can be made. Telephone cards are sold by post offices, kiosks and tobacconists.

European mobile phones work everywhere on Madeira and Porto Santo via the Portuguese networks. It is still cheaper to send a text message than to make a call by mobile. If you are staying in Portugal for more than a short period, it is worth buying a prepaid card (usually with a start-off credit).

Country codes: UK 0044, Ireland 00353, USA 001. For calls to Madeira/Porto Santo 00 351.

POST

A red and white sign with a horse rider and the letters CTT identifies post offices. Their usual hours are Mon–Fri 9am–12.30pm and 2–5.30pm. The main post office in Funchal *(Av. Zarco)* opens Mon–Fri 9am–8pm and Sat 9am–1pm. Stamps *(selos)* are also on sale in licensed bars, newsagents and kiosks.

Postcards and letters up to 20 g within Europe need a stamp for 0.68 euros.

PUBLIC TRANSPORT

Almost any place on Madeira and the great majority of sights can be reached by bus. *See the back flap of this book for a map of the routes.*

A little electric bus *(Linha Eco)* runs around the centre of Funchal – and there's no charge. Bus tickets can generally be purchased from the driver, but they are much cheaper at the kiosks of the various bus companies. For Funchal it is worth getting the electronic 'Giros' for 1 euro per journey (plus 0.50 euros once only for the ticket itself). You load a credit at the machine before the journey, or get the 7-day pass (17 euros) for all routes in the city. Night buses can be used only with the standard ticket (1.80 euros).

Madeira has no unified bus network but instead a number of bus operators who are responsible for different regions. In the Funchal area the bus company is *Horários do Funchal (www.horariosdofunchal.pt,* with bus timetable for the Funchal region*), EACL (www.eacl.pt)* links the island's capital to Caniço, *Rodoeste* has the routes to the west of Madeira *(www.rodoeste.pt)* and SAM the east *(www.sam.pt)*. There is a kind of central bus station on the edge of the old quarter of Funchal: most buses depart between the cable-car terminus and Praça da Autonomia. Others stop along Avenida do Mar, as do many private hotel shuttle buses and the airport bus *(aerobus)*, which takes 20–30 minutes from the airport to the hotel zone (5 euros). A TAP flight ticket takes you into town free of charge.

TAXIS

Taxis have a meter for journeys in Funchal, and always have a copy of the tariff for reference. The minimum fare is 2 euros. To call a taxi in Funchal dial *tel. 2 91 76 44 76,* or ask the hotel reception desk. For tours of the island, the price should be between 50 and 100 euros. Trips to and from the airport cost 20–30 euros, depending on the distance. Overland journeys are charged according to a list of fixed prices, even though the meter is not switched on.

TIME

Madeira is in the Greenwich Mean Time zone. The clocks are put forward one hour from late March to late October, so visitors from the British Isles do not need to reset their watches.

TIPPING

In restaurants it is usual to round up the amount on the bill or add 5–10 per cent as a tip. To do this simply leave some coins on the plate on which the bill is brought in a restaurant or café. Taxi drivers, hotel chambermaids, porters, tour guides and shoe cleaners are also pleased if they can top up their usually modest earnings with a tip.

WATER

The tap water is safe to drink but tastes slightly chlorinated and has often been chemically treated. There is no reason not to use it for cleaning your teeth, but it is advisable to buy drinking water in a supermarket, e.g. as a five-litre canister.

WEATHER IN FUNCHAL

	Jan	Feb	March	April	May	June	July	Aug	Sept	Oct	Nov	Dec
Daytime temperatures in °C/°F	16/61	16/61	16/61	17/63	18/64	20/68	21/70	22/72	22/72	21/70	19/66	17/63
Nighttime temperatures in °C/°F	13/55	13/55	14/57	14/57	15/59	18/64	19/66	20/68	19/66	18/64	16/61	14/57
Sunshine hours/day	5	6	6	7	8	6	8	8	7	7	5	5
Precipitation days/month	7	6	7	4	2	1	0	1	2	7	7	7
Water temperature in °C/°F	18/64	17/63	17/63	17/63	18/64	20/68	21/70	22/72	23/73	22/72	20/68	19/66

USEFUL PHRASES PORTUGUESE

PRONUNCIATION

To help you say the Portuguese words we have added a simple pronunciation guide in square brackets and an apostrophe ' before the syllable that is stressed. Note the following sounds shown in the pronunciation guide:
"zh" like the "s" in "pleasure", "ng" indicates a nasal sound at the end of a word (i.e. not with distinct consonants as in English) , e.g. "não" is shown as "nowng", "ee" as in "fee", "ai" as in "aisle", "oo" as in "zoo"

IN BRIEF

Yes/No/Maybe	sim [seeng]/não [nowng]/talvez [tal'vesh]
Please	se faz favor [se fash fa'vor]
Thank you	obrigado (m)/obrigada (f) [obri'gadoo/obri'gada]
Sorry/ Excuse me, please	Desculpa! [dish'kulpa]/Desculpe! [dish'kulp]
May I ...?/ Pardon?	Posso ...? ['possoo]/ Como? ['komoo]
I would like to ...	Queria ... [ke'ria]
Have you got ...?	Tem ...? [teng]
How much is ...	Quanto custa ...? ['kwantoo 'kooshta]
good/bad/broken/ doesn't work	bem [beng]/mal [mal]/estragado [ishtra'gadoo]/ não funciona [nowng fung'siona]
too much/much/little	demais [de'maish]/muito ['mooitoo]/pouco ['pokoo]
all/nothing	tudo ['toodoo]/nada ['nada]
Help!/Attention!/Caution!	Socorro! [soo'korroo]/Atenção! [atten'sowng]
ambulance	ambulância [amboo'langsia]
police/fire brigade	polícia [pu'lisia]/bombeiros [bom'beyroosh]
prohibition/forbidden	interdição [interdi'sowng]/proibido [prooi'bidoo]
danger/dangerous	perigo [pe'rigoo]/perigoso [peri'gosoo]

GREETINGS, FAREWELL

Good morning!/afternoon!/evening!/night!	Bom dia! [bong 'dia]/Bom dia! [bong 'dia]/ Boa tarde! ['boa 'tard]/Boa noite! ['boa 'noyt]
Hello!/Goodbye!	Olá! [o'la]/Adeus! [a'dy-oosh]
See you	Cião! [chowng]
My name is ...	Chamo-me ... ['shamoo-me]
What's your name?	Como se chama? ['komoo se 'shama]
	Como te chamas? ['komoo te 'shamas]
I'm from ...	Sou de ... [so de]

Falas português?

"Do you speak Portuguese?" This guide will help you to say the basic words and phrases in Portuguese.

DATE & TIME

Monday/Tuesday	segunda-feira [se'goonda 'feyra]/terça-feira ['tersa 'feyra]
Wednesday/Thursday	quarta-feira ['kwarta 'feyra]/quinta-feira ['kinta 'feyra]
Friday/Saturday	sexta-feira ['seshta 'feyra]/sábado ['sabadoo]
Sunday	domingo [doo'mingoo]
today/tomorrow/	hoje ['ozhe]/amanhã [amman'ya]/
yesterday	ontem ['onteng]
hour/minute	hora ['ora]/minuto [mi'nootoo]
day/night/week	dia [dia]/noite [noyt]/semana [se'mana]
month/year	mês [meysh]/ano ['anoo]
What time is it?	Que horas são? [ke 'orash sowng]
It's three o'clock	São três horas. [sowng tresh 'orash]
It's half past three	São três e meia. [sowng tresh i 'meya]

TRAVEL

open/closed	aberto [a'bertoo]/fechado [fe'shadoo]
entrance	entrada [en'trada]
exit	saída [sa'ida]
departure/arrival	partida [par'tida]/chegada [she'gada]
toilets/restrooms/	sanitários [sanni'tariush]/
ladies/gentlemen	senhoras [sen'yorash]/senhores [sen'joresh]
(no) drinking water	água (não) potável ['agwa (nowng) po'tavel]
Where is ...?/Where are ...?	Onde é ...? ['onde e]/Onde são ...? ['onde sowng]
left/right	à esquerda [a ish'kerda]/à direita [a dee'reyta]
straight ahead/back	em frente [eng 'frente]/para atrás ['para'trash]
bus	autocarro [auto'karroo]
stop	paragem [pa'razheng]
parking lot	estacionamento [eshtassiona'mentoo]
street map/map	mapa ['mappa]/mapa da cidade ['mappa da see'dad]
train station/	estação ferroviária [eshta'sowng ferrovi'aria]/
harbour/airport	porto ['portoo]/aeroporto [a-eyro'portoo]
schedule/ticket	horário [o'rariyu]/bilhete [bil'yet]
single/return	só ida [so 'ida]/ida e volta ['ida i 'vollta]
train/platform	comboio [kom'boyoo]/linha ['linya]
I would like to rent ...	Gostaria de alugar ... [goshta'ria de alloo'gar]
a car/a bicycle/	um carro [oong 'karroo]/uma bicicleta [ooma
a boat	bissi'kletta]/um barco [oong 'barkoo]
petrol/gas station/	bomba de gasolina ['bomba de gaso'lina]/
petrol/gas / diesel	petróleo [pe'troleo]/gasóleo [ga'soleo]
breakdown/repair shop	avaria [ava'ria]/garagem [ga'razheng]

FOOD & DRINK

Could you please book a table for tonight for four?	Se faz favor, pode reservar-nos para hoje à noite uma mesa para quatro pessoas. [se fash fa'vor, 'pode reser'varnoosh 'para 'oshe ah noit ooma 'mesa 'para 'kwatroo pe'ssoash]
The menu, please	A ementa, se faz favor. [a i'menta, se fash fa'vor]
bottle/glass	garrafa [gar'raffa]/copo ['koppoo]
salt/pepper/sugar	sal [sall]/pimenta [pi'menta]/açúcar [a'ssookar]
vinegar/oil	vinagre [vi'nagre]/azeite [a'zeite]
milk/cream/lemon	leite ['leyte]/natas ['natash]/limão [li'mowng]
with/without ice/sparkling	com [kong]/sem [seng] gelo ['zheloo]/gás [gash]
vegetarian/allergy	vegetariano/-a [vezhetari'anoo/-a]/alergia [aller'zhia]
May I have the bill, please?	A conta, se faz favor. [a 'konta, se fash fa'vor]

SHOPPING

Where can I find...?	Quero ... ['keroo]/Procuro ... [pro'kooroo]
pharmacy/chemist	farmácia [far'massia]/drogaria [droga'ria]
baker/market	padaria [pada'ria]/mercado [mer'kadoo]
shopping centre	centro comercial ['sentroo kommer'ssial]
100 grammes/1 kilo	cem gramas [seng 'grammash]/um quilo [oong 'kiloo]
expensive/cheap/price	caro ['karoo]/barato [ba'ratoo]/preço ['pressoo]
more/less	mais [maish]/menos ['menoosh]

ACCOMMODATION

I have booked a room	Reservei um quarto. [rezer'vey oong 'kwartoo]
Do you have any ... left?	Ainda tem ...? [a'inda teng]
single room	um quarto individual [oong 'kwartoo individu'al]
double room	um quarto de casal [oong 'kwartoo de ka'sal]
breakfast/	pequeno-almoço [pe'kaynoo al'mossoo]/
half board/	meia pensão ['meya pen'sowng]/
full board (American plan)	pensão completa [pen'sowng kom'pleta]
shower/sit-down bath	ducha [doosha]/banho ['banyoo]
balcony/terrace	varanda [va'randa]/terraço [ter'rassoo]
key/room card	chave ['chav-e]/cartão [kar'towng]
luggage/suitcase	bagagem [ba'gazheng]/mala ['mala]/saco ['sakoo]

BANKS, MONEY & CREDIT CARDS

bank/ATM	banco ['bankoo]/multibanco ['multibankoo]
pin code	código pessoal ['kodigoo pesso'al]
cash/	em dinheiro [eng din'yeyroo]/
credit card	com cartão de crédito [kong kar'towng de 'kreditoo]
note/coin	nota ['nota]/moeda [mo'ayda]

USEFUL PHRASES

HEALTH

doctor/dentist/paediatrician	médico ['medikoo]/dentista [den'tishta]/pediatra [pedi'atra]
hospital/emergency clinic	hospital [oshpi'tal]/urgências [oor'zhensiash]
fever/pain	febre ['feybre]/dores ['doresh]
diarrhoea/nausea	diarreia [diar'reya]/enjoo [eng'zho]
sunburn	queimadura [keyma'doora]
inflamed/injured	inflamado [infla'madoo]/ferido [fe'ridoo]
plaster/bandage	penso ['pengshoo]/ligadura [liga'doora]
tablet	comprimido [kompri'midoo]

POST, TELECOMMUNICATIONS & MEDIA

stamp/letter/postcard	selo ['seloo]/carta ['karta]/postal [posh'tal]
I'm looking for a prepaid card for my mobile	Procuro um cartão SIM para o meu telemóvel. [pro'kooroo oong kar'towng sim 'para oo meyoo tele'movel]
Where can I find internet access?	Onde há acesso à internet? ['onde a a'ssessoo a 'internet]
computer/battery/rechargeable battery	computador [kompoota'dor]/pilha ['pilya]/bateria [bate'ria]
internet connection	ligação à internet [liga'sowng a 'internet]

LEISURE, SPORTS & BEACH

beach/sunshade/lounger	praia ['praya]/guarda-sol [gwarda 'sol]/espreguiçadeira [eshpregissa'deyra]
low tide/high tide/current	maré baixa [ma're 'baisha]/maré alta [ma're alta]/corrente [kor'rente]

NUMBERS

0	zero ['zeroo]	20	vinte [veengt]
1	um, uma ['oong, 'ooma]	21	vinte e um ['veengt e 'oong]
2	dois, duas ['doysh, 'dooash]	30	trinta ['treengta]
3	três [tresh]	40	quarenta [kwa'renta]
4	quatro ['kwatroo]	50	cinquenta [seeng'kwengta]
5	cinco ['seengkoo]	100	cem ['seng]
6	seis ['seysh]	200	duzentos [doo'zentoosh]
7	sete ['set]	1000	mil ['meel]
8	oito ['oytoo]	2000	dois mil ['doysh meel]
9	nove ['nov]	10.000	dez mil ['desh meel]
10	dez ['desh]	½	um meio [oong 'meyoo]
11	onze ['ongs]	¼	um quarto [oong 'kwartoo]

ROAD ATLAS

The green line ▬ indicates the Trips & tours (p. 90–95)
The blue line ▬ indicates the Perfect route (p. 30–31)

All tours are also marked on the pull-out map

Photo: The village of Boaventura in the north of Madeira

Exploring Madeira

The map on the back cover shows how the area has been sub-divided

2 km
1,24 mi

Ponta do

1

Salão
Santa
Pombais

Achada Grande
ER 1

Quebrada Nova

Achada da Arruda

2

**Achadas
da Cruz**
675
Achada do Pinheira
Cova
370

Fajã Nova

Lombo da Terça
Terça
935

Lombo da Aze

N. Sra. da
Bos Morte
Cabo
Lombada Velha
10
13
Chão do Covão

Fonte d
1022

392

Ribeira
da Vaca
Serrado
Cab. de Aposento
767
1060

3

Ponta do
Pargo

Pedregal
ER 101

Cab. das Covas
913

E

Favas
392
Salão de B.

Ponta do Pargo

Pico da Pedreira
1093

Levada Nova

Salão de C.
682
Lombo do Meio
812

116

Fajã Grande
Fajã Pequena
Lombadinha

Corujeira de Fora
774

Alto da Ponta
998
1008
do Pargo
Passada Vermelha

4

537
Amparo
Lombo

Lombo dos Verdes

Pico da Cova Grande
887

dos Câmbios

1000

Mar

**Achada
do Mestre**

Achada do Mestre
8.5
730
Lombada dos Marinheiros

Ribeira

Lombos
992

Poiso da Faja
876
da Ovelha

Cab. da Roseira

19,5

Macapez

**Fajã da
Ovelha**

São João
São Lourenço

Lombo de S. João

Ribeira das Fajas

Ribeiro do Ch

Lombo da Raposeira

Lombo do

5

Lombada dos Cedros
3,4
1,5
ER 101
768

Raposeira do Serrado
ER 223
531
Ribeira das Galinhas

Raposeira
do Lugarinho
Malhada
VR 3

Lombo da

4,5
Serrado
da Cruz
Lagoa
Raposeira
599

Prazeres

6

Paúl do Mar
Igreja
Quebrada
Lombo da Rocha

Estacada
Carreira
64
ER 22

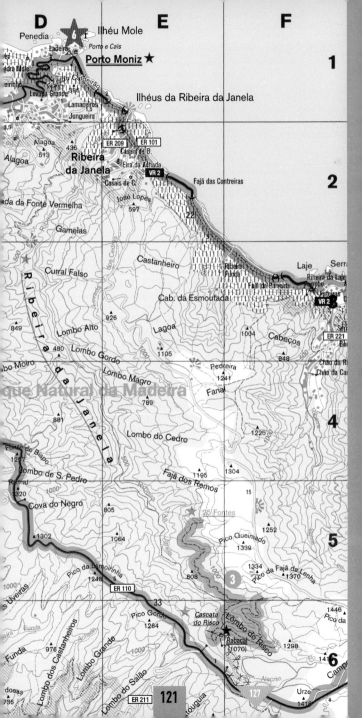

D   E   F

Ilhéu Mole

Penedia

Ladeiros

Porto e Cais

Porto Moniz ★

1

Fonte Calheirão

Levada Grande

Ilhéus da Ribeira da Janela

Lamaceiros

Junqueira

ER 209 · ER 101

Casais da B.

Alagoa

Alagoa 513

Ribeira da Janela

436

Eira da Achada

Casais de C.

VR 2

Fajã das Contreiras

2

da da Fonte Vermelha

José Lopes 597

Gamelas

Castanheiro

Ribeir

Fajã do Parreiral

Laje · Serra

Ribeira da Laje

Penedo

VR 2

Curral Falso

Cab. da Esmoutada

926

849

Lombo Alto

Lagoa

1004

Cabeços

ER 221

480

Lombo Gordo

1105

849

Chão da Pa

bo Moiro

Lombo Magro

Pedreira 1241

Chão da Ca

que Natural da Madeira

789

Fanal

881

Lombo do Cedro

1225

4

Fonte do Bispo 1297

Dombo de S. Pedro

Faja dos Remos 1195

1304

Ramal 1320

15

Cova do Negro

805

25 Fontes

1302

1064

1252

Pico Queimado 1339

5

Pico da Lamoirinha 1248

808

1334

Pico da Fajã da Lenha 1370

3

ER 110

33

1446

Pico d

Uveiras

Pico Gordo 1264

Cascata do Risco

Lombo do Risco

1298

14

Funda

976

Lombo dos Castanheiros

Rabaçal (1070)

6

dosas 796

Lombo Grande

Lombo do Salão

Alecrim

Urze 1418

Camp

ER 211

121

127

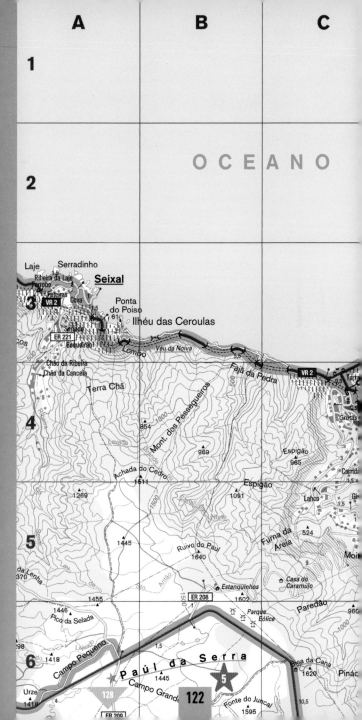

	A	B	C
1			
2		O C E A N O	

3

Laje
Serradinho
Ribeira da Laje
Farrobo
Seixal
Feiteiras
Cova
VR 2
Ponta
do Poiso
61
Serrado
Ilhéu das Ceroulas
ER 221
Boqueirão
Lombo
Veu da Noiva
5.5
VR 2

4

Chão da Ribeira
Chão da Cancela
Fajã da Pedra
Terra Chã
854
Mont. dos Pessegueiros
969
Espigão
965
Grutas
Levada
Achada do Cedro
1511
Espigão
1091
Lahço
5
Corrida
1269
Atube

5

1445
Ruivo do Paul
1640
Furna da
Areia
524
Moi
da Lenha
370
Sto.
Casa do
Caramujo
9
1455
Estanquinhos
ER 208
1602
Paredão
960
1446
Antão
Parque
Eólico
Pico da Selada
1500
1000

6

98
1418
Campo Pequena
Lajeado
Bica da Cana
1620
Urze
Paúl da Serra
1445
5
Pinác
1418
128
Campo Grande
122
Fonte do Juncal
10,5
ER 209
1595

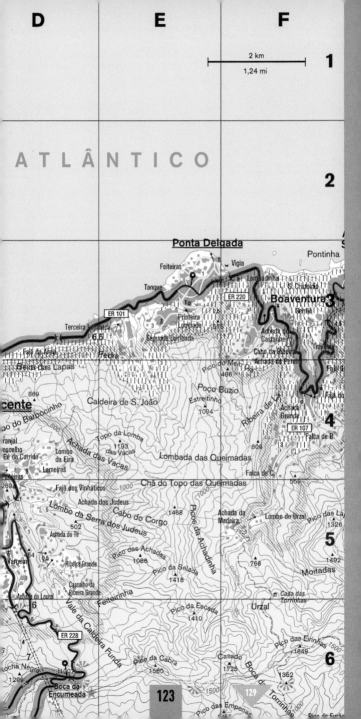

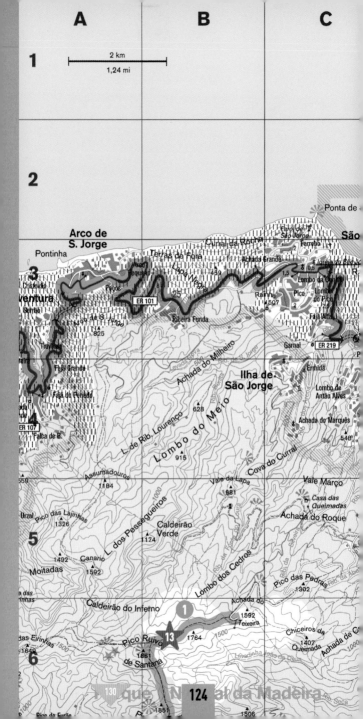

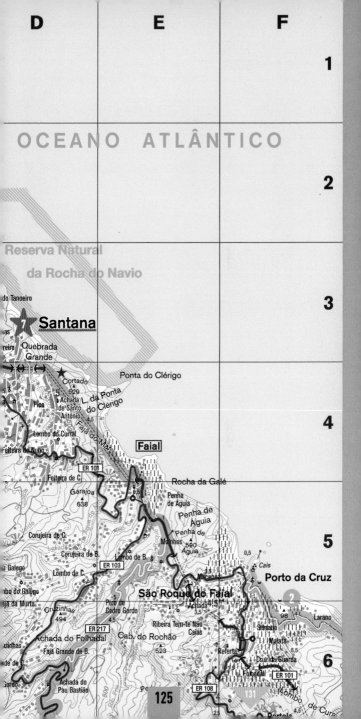

OCEANO ATLÂNTICO

Reserva Natural
da Rocha do Navio

do Tanoeiro

7 ⭐ **Santana**

Quebrada
Grande

Cortado
629

Achada
de Santo
António

Pico

L. da Ponta
do Clérigo

Ponta do Clérigo

Faial

Lombo do Curral

Feiteira de Nuno

ER 101

Feiteira de C.

Rocha da Galé

Garajoa
638

Penha
de Águia

Corujeira de C.

Penha de
Águia

Corujeira de B.

Lombo de B.

ER 103

Penha de
Águia

Moinhos
590

0,5

Cais

0,5

Lombo de C.

Galego

Macagá

Porto da Cruz

Faja do Galego

São Roque do Faial

2

98

Larano

Faja da Murta

Cruzinhas
494

Pico de
Cedro Gordo

Achada
415

ja da Murta

ER 217

Ribeira Tem-te Não
Caías

Cab. do Rochão
529

Serrado

Matata
6,5

Referta

Achada do Folhadal

zinhas

Fajã Grande da B.

ER 108

Cruz da Guarda

Folhadal

ER 101

de de

Achada do
Pau Bastião

125

131

Lombo de Cura

1

2

3

4

5

6

D   E   F

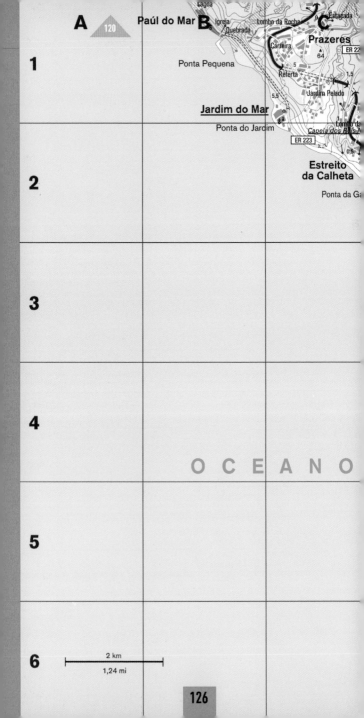

A 120

Paúl do Mar B Igreja
Quebrada

Lombo da Rocha

C Estacada

Prazeres

ER 22

Carreira

64

1

Ponta Pequena

Referta

5

1,5

Jardim Pelado

5,5

Jardim do Mar

Ponta do Jardim

4

Lombo da

Capela dos Reis

ER 223

0,5

**Estreito
da Calheta**

2

Ponta da Ga

3

4

O C E A N O

5

6

2 km

1,24 mi

D   **E**   **F**

1

2

3

4

5

6

Lombo do Ca...
Lombo ...
Lombo do Salão
ER 211
Urze
1418
121
1418
1096
Lombo da Atouguia
Achadinha
Cha da Quebrada
Cova do Birão
1174
957
Lombo do Lameiro
Lombo do Doutor
6
Lombo dos Reis
Lombo das Laranjeiras
489
Lombo dos Faias
999
Lombo do Brasil
Lombo do Salão
ER 222
Florenças
Lombo do Salão
Lombo da Atouguia
Arco da Calheta
Amoreiras
224
Chão
846
Cales e Chada
ER 209
Lombo do Doutor
Cova do Arco
Confre...
VR 3
Achada da Silva
ER 101
Lombada do Loreto
Paredes
842
Macapez
Ledo
0,5
Amoreiras
Barreiro e Feiteiras
Arco da Calheta
Faja e Eiras
ER 222
225
Ladeira e Lamaceiros
Carvalhal e Carreta
Achada e Le... do Poiso
5,5
1,5
Capela de N. Sra. da Vida
Salões
479
Levada da Madalena
Madalena do Mar
Salões
3,5
Vale e Cova do Pico
Lomb...
Ca...
15
VR 3
Lombo do Outeiro
Passo
Lo...
Outeiro
Vol...
Cais
Anjos
303
ER 101

T L Â N T I C O   **Ponta d...**

Paúl da Serra

A   **B**   ⭐5   **C**

Campo Pec
▲1418
Urze
1418

122

Campo Grande
1445

Bica da Cana
1620

Pinác

1

ER 209

Loiral
1415

Loiral

1428

Cascalbo

Fonte do Juncal
1595

10,5

ER 110

Pedras
1615

Casa do
go M
▲1246

Faja do Carro

Lombo do Mouro

2

▲999

Confrarias
1333

885

Pico da Sra. da Ajuda
1264

1369

ER 209

Lombo Galego

836

Lombo das Torres

1007

842

Lombo de S. João

Lombo das Terças

736

Lombo da Banda d'Além

3

Achada e Levada
do Poiso

604

Pomar de D. João

Ribeira da Tábua
887

da Madalena

Lombo das Canhas

Salão

Vala Zimbreiro

688

Canhas

do Outeiro

Lombo da Piedade

Jangão

500

VR 4

eiro

Voltinhas

Anjos
303

Lombada

5

2,5

Faja do Trigo

Faja
da Fit

4

ER 101

1,5

Candelária

3,5

Livramento
226

0,5

ER 222

Corujeira

Apresentação

5

São Joã

Lugar de B.

Tábua

Praia

1,5

Alhos
(369)

Vala

2,5

ER 227

1,5

VR 3

0,5

Ponta do Sol

Pedra de
Nossa Senhora

⭐ **Ribeira Brava**

Cais

3

Nossa Sra
da Gloria

5

O C E A N O   A T L Â N T I C O

6

2 km

1,24 mi

128

D Rocha Negra 1289

100

E

Pico da Cabra 1558

Casado B 1725

1649

F 352

Boca da Encumeada

123

ER 228

5 Achada 917

Fajã das Éguas

Vinháticos do Moira

Pousada dos Vinháticos

597

VR 4 796

Terra Grande

Serra de Água

Lombo do Moleiro

Poço

Pico das Empenas 1455

Pico do Furão **1** 1

Fajã dos Cardos

Pico do Cerco 1654

Cumeal

Fajã Escura

Poço do Bor 149

Fenda do Ferreiro

Pico do Melo-Vintém 1018

Boca do Cerro

1443

780

Achada **2**

726

Passo de Ares

Cristo do Espigão 1311

★★ **Curral das Freiras**

Casas Proximas

1 Murteiras

Capela 3.5

1436

Terra-Chã

Balseiros

Pico do Serraço 1088

Eira do Grilo 1147

Pico Redondo 1155

Pico da Malhada 1235

Seara Velha

Lombo Chão

Espigão

Fontes

40

852

Lombo Furado

Lombo do Covão ou Estrebaria

Pico da Meroiço

1181

Achada

Serra da Eira da Laje

6 1054

Lombo da Partilha **3**

Terreiros

Choro

779

Lugar da Serra 694

Eira das Moças

Ribeira Funda

Cabo Podão

Marco e Fonte da Pedra

da Coroa 786

Cruz das Moças 956

Fontainhas

Pau Branco

Cabo Podão

Jardim da Serra

Romeiras

Rochas Altas 1.5

Fontes

1.5

Castelejo 2.5

852

Marinheira

Maçapez

Conqueira

Foro

Igreja

Barreiros

Covão

4

749

Achada do Campanário

Nogueira

Garachico

Estreito de Câmara de Lobos

Campanário

Igreja 6.5

Tranqual

Quinta Grande

ER 229 (Igreja)

4.5

Vargem

Covão e Panasque

Ribeiro Real

Igreja

Cruz

Caldeira

2.5

Quinta do Leme

Saraiva

261

5 oure

VR 1

Galo

631

13

Fajã dos Padres

Fajã dos Asnos

Cabo Girão

Ribeiro de Alforra e Fonte Garcia

Rancho

Caminho Grande

Ribeiro de Alforra

Serrado de Adega

ER 229

Torre

Pamieira

Lombada

0.5

Vila

Pé do Pico

2.5

251

★ **CÂMARA DE LOBOS**

Cais

53

Vitoria

Espírito Santo e Calçada

6

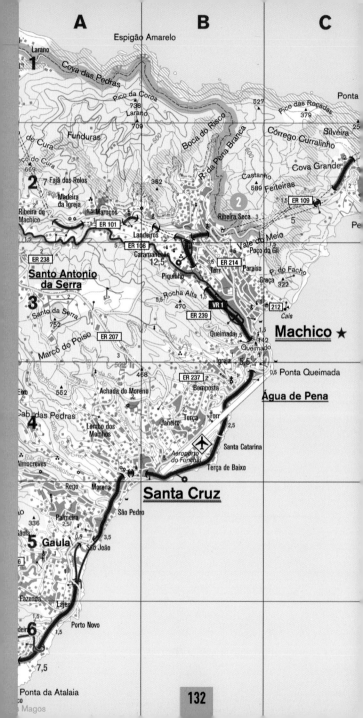

A **B** **C**

1 Larano
Espigão Amarelo
Cova das Pedras
Pico da Coroa 738
Larano 709
Ponta
Pico das Roçadas 527 379
25

de Cura 669
Funduras
Boca do Risco
R. da Pena Branca
Córrego Curralinho
Silveira
Cova Grande
2

2 7 Fajã dos Rolos
Madeira da Igreja
Ribeira de Machico
1,5 Marocos
ER 101
382
Castanho 589 Feiteiras
Caníco
1,5 ER 109
5
Pe
1,5
Landeiros
ER 108
Ribeira Seca 3
Vale do Meio
2

3 ER 238
Santo Antonio da Serra
Caramanchão 12,5
Rocha Alta 5,5 470
ER 239
Piquinho
VR 1
Poço do Gil
4,5
ER 214
Torr
Paraíso
Graça
P. do Facho 322
212
Cais
Machico ★
Santo da Serra 752
Marco do Poiso
ER 207
Queimada 5
1,5
142
1,5

4 468
ER 237 2
Bemposta
Achada do Moreno
Janeiro
Terça
Torr
2
2
Lombo dos Moinhos
552
Eixo
Cab. das Pedras
Almocreves
Aeroporto do Funchal ✈
Queimado
Igreja 5,5
0,5 Ponta Queimada
Água de Pena
2,5
Santa Catarina
Terça de Baixo

5 Rege
Morena
São Pedro
Santa Cruz
336 Palmeira 2,5
Gaula
São João 3,5
6
1

6 Fazenda
Lajes
1,5
Porto Novo
1,5
deira
7,5
Ponta da Atalaia
s Magos

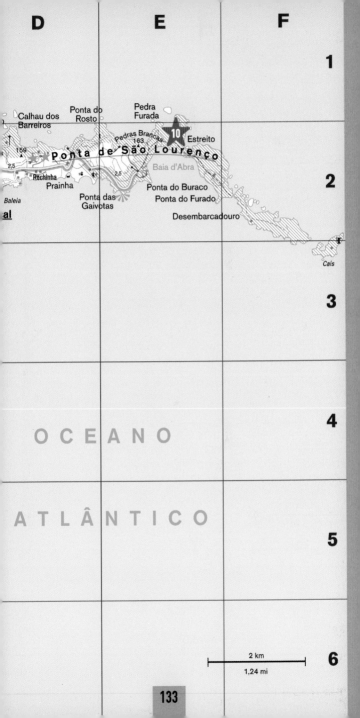

D E F

1

Calhau dos Barreiros Ponta do Rosto Pedra Furada

159 Pedras Brancas 163 Estreito
Ponta de São Lourenço
2,5 Baia d'Abra
2,5

Rochinha Prainha Ponta das Gaivotas Ponta do Buraco
Baleia Ponta do Furado
al Desembarcadouro

2

Cais

3

O C E A N O

4

A T L Â N T I C O

5

2 km
1,24 mi

6

133

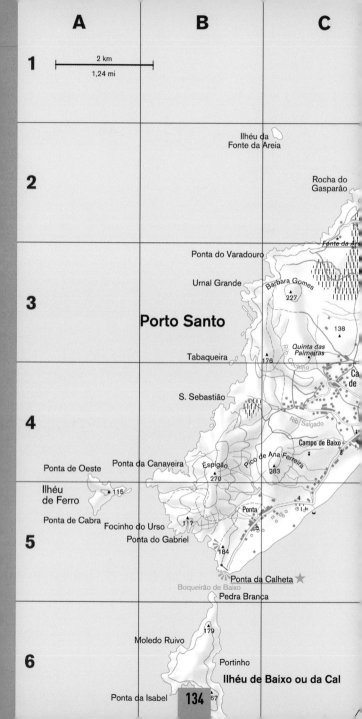

	A	B	C
1			
2		Ilhéu da Fonte da Areia	Rocha do Gasparão
3	**Porto Santo**	Ponta do Varadouro Urnal Grande Tabaqueira	Fonte da Are Barbara Gomes 227 138 Quinta das Palmeiras 176 Ca de
4	Ponta de Oeste	S. Sebastião Ponta da Canaveira	Rib Salgado Campo de Baixo
5	Ilhéu de Ferro 115 Ponta de Cabra	Espigão 270 Focinho do Urso 117 Ponta do Gabriel 184	Pico de Ana Ferreira 283 Ponta 4
6		Ponta da Calheta ★ Boqueirão de Baixo Pedra Branca Moledo Ruivo 179 Portinho Ponta da Isabel **134** 67	**Ilhéu de Baixo ou da Cal**

2 km
1,24 mi

D **E** **F**

Ilhéu
de Fora

Baixa do Meio **1**

Baixa dos Barbeiros

Focinho da Forte

Ilhéu das Cenouras

Furnas das
Amasiadas

Rib. da Pedregos

120

4,5

1,5

Pico das Urzes

450

440

Rib. da

Serra de Dentro

Serra de Dentro

2

Camacha

Pico do Facho

517

Pico do Castelo

437

2

Pico do Concelho

324

Ponta dos Ferreiros **3**

3

Serra de Fora

1,5

Estreito

Capela de
Na. Sra. da
Graça

Dragoal

1,5

Casinhas

163

Barroca

Portela

275

4

Rib. do Galhau

Penêdo

Pico do Macarico

285

1,5

lões

11

2

Mus. de Cristóvão ★

Porto
de Abrigo

Ponta
da Galé

Vila Baleira
(Porto Santo)

Boqueirão de Cima

119

Ilhéu de Cima **4**

5

O C E A N O

A T L Â N T I C O

Tumbai

6

135

KEY TO ROAD ATLAS

Autobahn · Gebührenpflichtige Anschlussstelle · Gebührenstelle · Anschlussstelle mit Nummer · Rasthaus mit Übernachtung · Raststätte · Kleinraststätte · Tankstelle · Parkplatz mit und ohne WC	Trento 11 ⓧ 🍴 🛏 Ⓟ Ⓟ	Motorway · Toll junction · Toll station · Junction with number · Motel · Restaurant · Snackbar · Filling-station · Parking place with and without WC
Autobahn in Bau und geplant mit Datum der Verkehrsübergabe	Datum Date	Motorway under construction and projected with completion date
Zweibahnige Straße (4-spurig)		Dual carriageway (4 lanes)
Fernverkehrsstraße · Straßennummern	14 E45	Trunk road · Road numbers
Wichtige Hauptstraße		Important main road
Hauptstraße · Tunnel · Brücke	)=(	Main road · Tunnel · Bridge
Nebenstraßen		Minor roads
Fahrweg · Fußweg		Track · Footpath
Wanderweg (Auswahl)	– – – – –	Tourist footpath (selection)
Eisenbahn mit Fernverkehr		Main line railway
Zahnradbahn, Standseilbahn		Rack-railway, funicular
Kabinenschwebebahn · Sessellift	o—o—o o—+—+	Aerial cableway · Chair-lift
Autofähre · Personenfähre	● ··········	Car ferry · Passenger ferry
Schifffahrtslinie		Shipping route
Naturschutzgebiet · Sperrgebiet	////// //////	Nature reserve · Prohibited area
Nationalpark · Naturpark · Wald		National park · natural park · Forest
Straße für Kfz. gesperrt	X X X X X	Road closed to motor vehicles
Straße mit Gebühr	·············	Toll road
Straße mit Wintersperre	–‖– –‖– XII-II	Road closed in winter
Straße für Wohnanhänger gesperrt bzw. nicht empfehlenswert	🚫 🚫 🚫 🚫	Road closed or not recommended for caravans
Touristenstraße · Pass	Weinstraße ⌒1510	Tourist route · Pass
Schöner Ausblick · Rundblick · Landschaftlich bes. schöne Strecke	🔆 🔆	Scenic view · Panoramic view · Route with beautiful scenery
Heilbad · Schwimmbad	⚓ –	Spa · Swimming pool
Jugendherberge · Campingplatz	△ △ ▲	Youth hostel · Camping site
Golfplatz · Sprungschanze	⌘ ⚐	Golf-course · Ski jump
Kirche im Ort, freistehend · Kapelle	ô ♦	Church · Chapel
Kloster · Klosterruine	♠ ♣	Monastery · Monastery ruin
Synagoge · Moschee	✡ ☪	Synagogue · Mosque
Schloss, Burg · Schloss-, Burgruine	♦ ♣	Palace, castle · Ruin
Turm · Funk-, Fernsehturm	⊥ 📡	Tower · Radio-, TV-tower
Leuchtturm · Kraftwerk	⊤ ♦	Lighthouse · Power station
Wasserfall · Schleuse	⌐ †	Waterfall · Lock
Bauwerk · Marktplatz, Areal	■ □	Important building · Market place, area
Ausgrabungs- u. Ruinenstätte · Bergwerk	∴ ⚒	Arch. excavation, ruins · Mine
Dolmen · Menhir · Nuraghen	π ◌ ♨	Dolmen · Menhir · Nuraghe
Hünen-, Hügelgrab · Soldatenfriedhof	☆ ⊞	Cairn · Military cemetery
Hotel, Gasthaus, Berghütte · Höhle	⌂ ∩	Hotel, inn, refuge · Cave

Kultur / Culture

Malerisches Ortsbild · Ortshöhe	**WIEN** (171)	Picturesque town · Elevation
Eine Reise wert	★★ **MILANO**	Worth a journey
Lohnt einen Umweg	★ **TEMPLIN**	Worth a detour
Sehenswert	<u>Andermatt</u>	Worth seeing

Landschaft / Landscape

Eine Reise wert	★★ <u>Las Cañadas</u>	Worth a journey
Lohnt einen Umweg	★ <u>Texel</u>	Worth a detour
Sehenswert	<u>Dikti</u>	Worth seeing

Ausflüge & Touren — **Trips & Tours**

Perfekte Route — **Perfect route**

MARCO POLO Highlight ★ **MARCO POLO Highlight**

INDEX

This index lists all places, islands and destinations mentioned in the guide.
Page numbers in bold type refer to the main entry.

WRITE TO US

e-mail: info@marcopologuides.co.uk

Did you have a great holiday?
Is there something on your mind?
Whatever it is, let us know!
Whether you want to praise, alert us to errors or give us a personal tip – MARCO POLO would be pleased to hear from you.
We do everything we can to provide the very latest information for your trip.

Nevertheless, despite all of our authors' thorough research, errors can creep in. MARCO POLO does not accept any liability for this. Please contact us by e-mail or post.

MARCO POLO Travel Publishing ltd
Pinewood, Chineham Business Park
Crockford Lane, Chineham
Basingstoke, Hampshire RG24 8AL
United Kingdom

PICTURE CREDITS
Cover Photograph: Câmara de Lobos, Cabo Girão (Huber: Gräfenhain)
G. Amberg (20, 49, 103); CS Hotels, Golf & Resorts (16 top); DuMont Bildarchiv: Leue (2 top, 3 centre, 4, 2 centre top, 7, 8, 23, 62, 70/71, 106 top, 106 bottom), Schwarzbach (101); Fresh Citrus: Joao Curiti (17 bottom); R. Hackenberg (9, 34, 43, 93); Huber: Gräfenhain (1 top, 2 centre bottom, 10/11, 32/33), Grandadam (26 r.), Schmid (102/103); ©iStockphoto.com: John Boylan (17 top); laif: Gonzalez (3 bottom, 80/81); S. Lier (1 bottom); Look: age fotostock (30 top, 107), Greune (96/97), TerraVista (30 bottom); Lúcia Sousa: Renato Nunes (16 centre); Marte Records: Rita Carmo (16 bottom); Mauritius: Coll (Klappe i., 64); T. Stankiewicz (6, 26 l., 28, 28/29, 38, 45; 52, 69, 82, 84, 86, 89, 99, 100/101, 102); vario images: Imagebroker (5); H. Wagner (Klappe r., 12, 15, 18/19, 21, 72, 90/91); T. P. Widmann (2 bottom, 3 top, 27, 47, 50/51, 60/61, 77); E. Wrba (24/25, 29, 36, 40/41, 54, 56, 57, 59, 67, 74, 79, 85, 94/95, 100, 118/119)

1st Edition 2012
Worldwide Distribution: Marco Polo Travel Publishing Ltd, Pinewood, Chineham Business Park, Crockford Lane, Basingstoke, Hampshire RG24 8AL, United Kingdom. Email: sales@marcopolouk.com
© MAIRDUMONT GmbH & Co. KG, Ostfildern
Chief editor: Marion Zorn
Author: Rita Henss; Co-author: Sara Lier; Editor: Nadia Al Kureischi
Programme supervision: Ann-Katrin Kutzner, Nikolai Michaelis, Silwen Randebrock
Picture editor: Nadia Al Kureischi, Gabriele Forst
What's hot: wunder media, Munich; Cartography road atlas: © MAIRDUMONT, Ostfildern
Cartography pull-out map: © MAIRDUMONT, Ostfildern
Design: milchhof : atelier, Berlin; Front cover, pull-out map cover, page 1: factor product munich
Translated from German by John Sykes, Cologne; editor of the English edition: Kathleen Becker, Lisbon
Prepress: BW-Medien GmbH, Leonberg
Phrase book in cooperation with Ernst Klett Sprachen GmbH, Stuttgart, Editorial by Pons Wörterbücher

DOS & DON'TS ☝

In Portuguese the polite phrase for 'don't' is por favor, não!

TOPLESS TOURISTS

Like other Portuguese and southern Europeans, for Madeirans it is important to be correctly clothed. Except on the beach, for men to walk around bare-chested is absolute taboo, and many residents of both towns and villages also react with displeasure when women are scantily dressed. For women to go topless is only acceptable around a hotel pool, if anywhere at all; in public pools and on the beach this really causes offence.

SAYING 'GRACIAS'

Most Portuguese can understand Spanish very well and know that 'Gracias' is easy to say for many tourists. But they are all the more pleased when visitors to the island make the effort to say 'thank you' in their own language: 'Obrigado!' (if the speaker is a man) or 'Obrigada!' (if à woman). Although the relations between Spain and Portugal are more relaxed than they often were in the past, the Portuguese don't like to be treated or spoken to as if they were Spanish.

HIGH HEELS

Madeira is not the right place for high heels. Even in Funchal, steep slopes and cobblestones make strolling around a little less smooth than it is in other cities. Trainers are more suitable than sandals or fashionable but unpractical footwear. If you go hiking in the mountains, don't fail to take proper walking boots that protect your ankles. The trails are often narrow and exposed to vertiginous drops. They are seldom maintained or fenced, and often slippery, which means real danger.

UNDERESTIMATING DISTANCES

Measured in miles or kilometres, the distances from A to B on Madeira seem modest. However, on almost any journey there are ravines and mountains in the way. The number of tunnels is increasing all the time, but in many places the journey still takes you over narrow, steep and winding roads. Fog, road blocks, rocks on the road (this is often the case, especially after heavy rain!) or slow-moving construction vehicles are further obstacles. Allow plenty of time when planning your tour.

CAREFUL WITH FIRE

Although Madeira is blessed with plentiful rainfall, in summer the vegetation can dry out to a surprising extent. A lighted cigarette carelessly thrown away or a badly tended barbecue can then cause a catastrophic fire. Especially in the sparsely populated west of the island, large-scale fires break out almost every year, and strong winds fan the flames.

WATCH OUT FOR TOUTS

There is a wide choice of restaurants in Funchal, especially in the old quarter. For all the competition, well-run establishments have no need for aggressive touts who wave the menu around and approach potential guests on the street. Say no in a friendly but firm manner.

WELCOME
to
'ILVER STREET
FARM

WELCOME
to
SILVER STREET
FARM

NICOLA DAVIES
illustrated by Katharine McEwen

**WALKER
BOOKS**

First published 2011 by Walker Books Ltd
87 Vauxhall Walk, London SE11 5HJ

2 4 6 8 10 9 7 5 3 1

Text © 2011 Nicola Davies
Illustrations © 2011 Katharine McEwen

The right of Nicola Davies and Katharine McEwen to be identified as
author and illustrator respectively of this work has been asserted by them in
accordance with the Copyright, Designs and Patents Act 1988.

This book has been typeset in Stempel Schneidler and Cows

Printed and bound in Great Britain
by Clays Ltd, St Ives plc

British Library Cataloguing in Publication Data:
a catalogue record for this book is available from the British Library

ISBN 978-1-4063-2059-6

www.walker.co.uk

For Joseph and Gabriel
and the real Flinty.

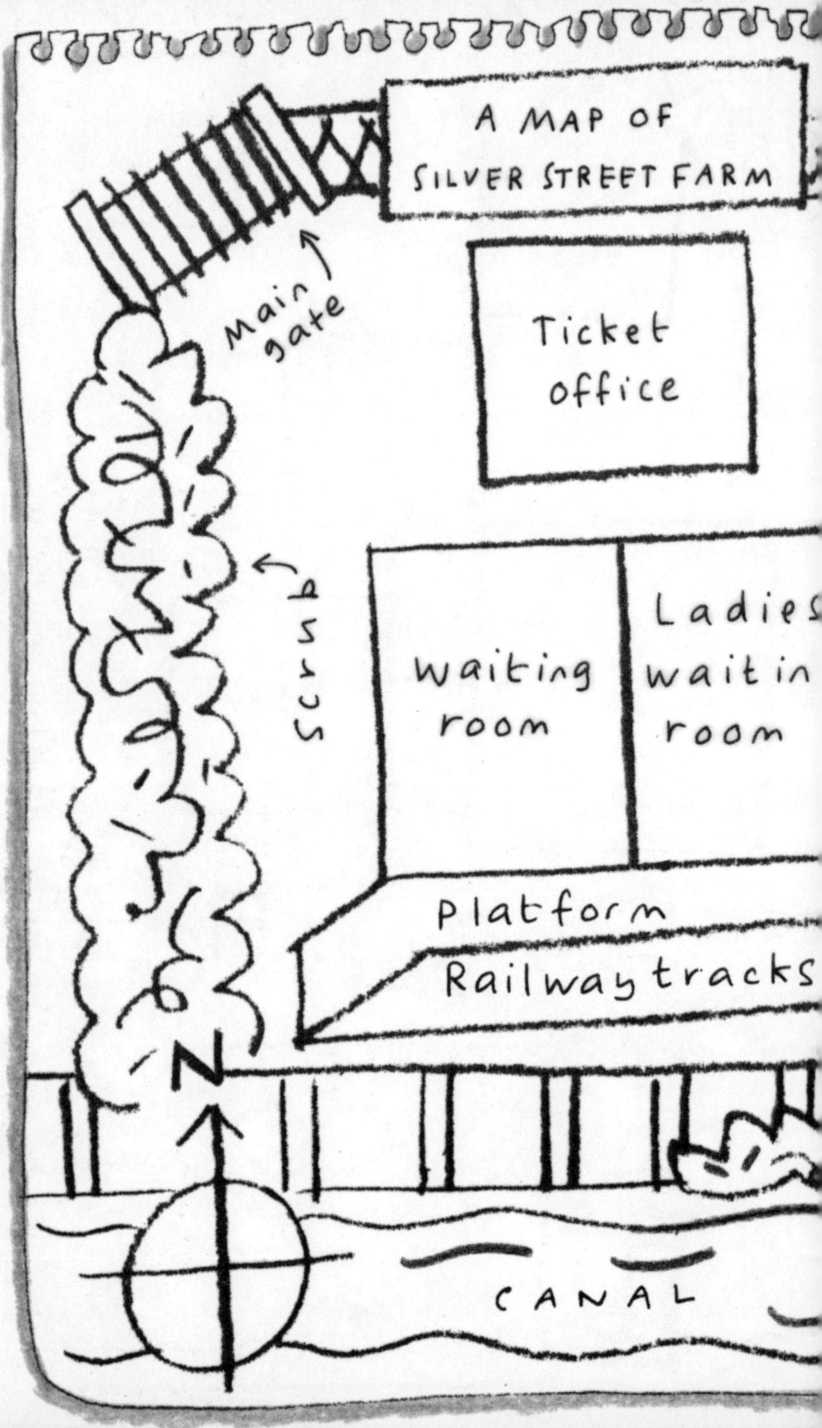

A MAP OF
SILVER STREET FARM

Ticket
office

Main gate

Scrub

Waiting
room

Ladies
waiting
room

Platform

Railway tracks

N

CANAL

Coal shed
Tool shed
fence
Out-house
out-house
Station master's office
Signal box
Old metal bridge

Chapter One

Gemma says that it started with eating jelly babies on the roundabout in the park. Karl says no, it started with Auntie Nat's poodles. But Meera knows that the *real* beginning of Silver Street was their very first day of Mrs Monty's class in Infants.

On that first day of school, the only children who weren't screaming, crying or having a nosebleed were a tall girl with ginger plaits, a quiet, skinny boy with dark hair, and Meera.

9

Mrs Monty led them to the play area in the corner of the classroom.

"Could you three play nicely with the toy town," she said, "while I sort everything else out? There are some farm animals too, in that red box."

Meera was lifting the lid off the red box almost before Mrs Monty had finished speaking; but she wasn't alone. The two other children were right beside her. Just like her, they weren't in the least bit interested in the posh toy town laid out all around them. It was the farm animals they wanted to play with.

"I'm Meera," said Meera, smiling shyly.

"I'm Gemma," said the tall girl with ginger plaits.

"I'm Karl," said the skinny boy very quietly. "Shall we play farms?"

For the rest of the day, whilst Mrs Monty wrestled with classroom chaos, the three new best friends built their first farm together. They got out all the animals, even the two cows with legs missing, the headless sheep and the chickens that had been painted pink. They made stables, stalls and sties from old cereal packets and new fences from lolly sticks and yellow wool. Very soon, fields and farm buildings, flocks of sheep and herds of cows and pigs had sprung up among the buildings and roads of the toy town.

The three children worked well together. Gemma liked the sheep and the chickens best; Karl didn't say much, but you could tell he liked the cows and the horses. Meera was always having ideas about what to do next, but Gemma and Karl didn't mind because she wasn't *really* bossy, and she had found the missing piglets at the bottom of the Lego box.

When Mrs Monty asked them to put the farm away at home time, the children were horrified.

"But I have to milk the cows in the morning," said Karl.

"And the sheep can't graze if they're in a *box*," said Gemma.

"But tomorrow the other children will want to play with the toy town," said Mrs Monty gently.

"They can play with the town *and* the farm, together!" said Gemma.

"You see," Meera explained, kindly, "it's a *city* farm. It fits in the city, just like the farm *we're* all going to have when we're older."

From that moment on, Meera, Gemma

and Karl planned their real city farm. They read books about farm animals and they went on every school trip and family outing they could to real farms to see and learn about real animals. All through Infants and right through to the last year of Juniors, the three friends planned – but still their city farm was just a dream. Until, that is, the day of the green jelly babies and Auntie Nat's poodles.

Chapter Two

Gemma and Karl were lying on the old roundabout in the park, eating jelly babies and looking up into the blue spring sky over Lonchester.

"Give us a push, Gem," said Karl. "We're stopping."

Gemma kicked out lazily at the concrete with one of her super-long legs and started the roundabout turning again.

Karl bit the head off a yellow jelly baby and sighed.

"Easter holidays at home with nothing to do but watch Auntie Nat read horoscopes…"

"I'd swap you a year with your auntie's horoscopes for two weeks with my spotty brother."

Gemma gave them another push and the roundabout creaked on. "Where is Meera, anyway?" she said through a mouthful of red jelly baby. "She said to meet at three o'clock and it's twenty past now."

"I'm right here!" Meera ran out of the trees and jumped onto the roundabout, sending it spinning madly. "And I've got some good news. This could be the year we start our farm!"

Either side of her, Karl and Gemma both groaned.

"Meera, we don't have any animals..." said Karl.

"And if we *did* have any animals, where would we keep them?" added Gemma. "My dad's tool-shed?"

"Or the balcony of Auntie's flat?" added Karl.

"But if we *did* have somewhere to keep them," said Meera, sitting bolt upright, "that would be a start, wouldn't it?"

"But finding somewhere is the difficult bit," said Karl, gloomily. "We've always known that."

"Well," said Meera, her eyes starting to sparkle, "I think I *have* found somewhere! My Auntie Priya works in the council offices and she told me about it. There's an old railway station down by the canal that's been closed for years. There are buildings to keep animals in and grassy bits for grazing. It sounds perfect."

"But the council would never let us have a place like that," said Gemma.

"It's probably just ruins covered in brambles," added Karl.

Meera ignored their objections. "It can't hurt to go and have a look though, can it?" she said.

But Gemma and Karl still looked doubtful.

"I know!" said Meera, leaping off the roundabout. "Let the jelly babies decide!" She snatched the bag from Gemma and struck a pose like an actor on a stage.

"I veel close my eyes. I veel hold out zee magical bag of jelly babies..." Meera paused dramatically. Peeping between her eyelashes, she could see that Karl and Gemma were now both watching her and starting to laugh – she'd *got* them! – "And if zee next baby I pull from zee bag eez *green* you veel be bound by jelly baby magic to accompany me on my quest for our farm!"

Meera pointed in Karl's direction.

"Drum roll please, Karl!"

Karl drummed his fingers on the old roundabout and Gemma provided a trumpet fanfare with a rolled-up newspaper.

Meera reached into the bag with her other hand, paused dramatically, and pulled out … a green jelly baby!

"Ta da!"

Karl and Gemma clapped and got off the roundabout. Sometimes, you just had to do what Meera wanted, even if you knew that the jelly baby *had* to be green, because none of them liked the lime-flavoured ones.

Chapter Three

Auntie Nat blinked. She looked at the screen again. It couldn't be true, could it?

"Adorable poodles. Two left. Bargain for quick sale."

The photo on the advert was terribly blurred, but then dogs moved around so much, didn't they? They'd be hard to photograph. She wrote down the number on the screen and, her heart pounding with excitement, reached for the phone...

Auntie Nat, or Natalia Konstantinovna Lebedeva, to give her her proper name, had always wanted a pair of white poodles, with ribbons tied into their woolly fur.

"I walk with them to shops," she would tell Karl in her heavy Russian accent, "and I look elegant, like models in magazine."

Then she'd walk across the sitting room, pretending to be a tall skinny model with two dogs on leads. This always made Karl and Auntie Nat laugh, because she was short and very, very round.

"When I'm rich and famous, Auntie," Karl always said, "I'll buy you two perfect little poodles."

"Ah, my Karl," she'd sigh, "you will have to be very rich. Poodles *so* expensive."

Poodles *were* so expensive, hundreds and hundreds of pounds. Every week, when she was reading her horoscope in *The Lonchester*

Herald and on the *Mythic Modes* website, she'd check online in case someone, somewhere, was selling a poodle for a price she could afford. But the stars always told her that wasn't going to happen. Until today.

"A long-held dream is closer than you think!" said her horoscope on the back page of *The City Gazette*.

The voice at the end of the phone line was gruff.

"Yeah, I still got the dogs," it said. "You got the money?"

"Hmmm," Auntie Nat thought to herself, "not a refined person. Not good enough to own fine poodles."

"Yes, yes," she said carefully, "I have money. Cash…"

"Right. Then meet me at the corner of

Milsom Street and Park Row in an hour."

He didn't even wait for her to reply. Perhaps the puppies were stolen. Auntie Nat pushed the worrying thought to the back of her mind and, thinking instead of what Karl would say when he got home and found two little poodle puppies in the flat, almost skipped down the corridor to the creaking, cranking old lift.

The man was definitely not a refined person. In fact, he looked as if he could do with a bath. What was more, he seemed to be in a great rush to get rid of the puppies. He shoved the box into Auntie Nat's hands and told her that the puppies were sleeping and that it would be better not to open the box until she got home. This had made her suspicious, but when she'd poked a finger in through an air hole in the pet carrier, she'd felt the warm, woolly fur. She handed over the money and hurried home.

Back in the flat, Auntie Nat dragged the pet carrier into the kitchen and sat down gratefully on a chair. She looked at it, but she didn't open it. Now that her long-held dream was about to come true as the horoscope had predicted, she realized that she didn't really know anything about poodles. They were cute and fluffy, but what did they eat? How did you train them? Where, she thought with sudden horror, did they "do their business"?

Inside the pet carrier, the pups were starting to wake up and move about. She would have to let them out. She opened the top of the carrier and two sweet, little, white woolly faces looked up at her and opened their mouths.

"Baa!" said the puppies. "Baaaaaaaa!"

Chapter Four

The old station was most definitely *not* open to visitors: the huge wrought-iron gates were closed with a giant chain and padlock and covered in signs that shouted fiercely, "No Entry!" and "Trespassers Will Be Prosecuted!" and, most worrying of all, "Danger! Guard Dogs Patrolling at All Times".

"We can't go in there!" said Karl.

"Yes, we can!" said Meera.

"What about the guard dogs?" asked Gemma.

"Oh, that's just for show," said Meera, waving her hands dismissively.

Karl, who was still small for his age, looked up at the gate.

"How will we get in?"

"Climb, of course. Durr!" said Meera.

Gemma laughed. "But you're rubbish at climbing, Meera!"

"That's where you come in, Daddy-Long-Legs. Get up there, Gemma!"

Gemma *was* the best climber of the three of them and she could never resist a challenge.

"OK. I'll get on top of the gate, then I'll help you guys up," she said, "and if we get put in jail, at least I won't have to spend all the holidays with my brother."

Once they were on top of the gates, it was easy to slide down the other side and start to explore. There were several old brick buildings, some with faded signs still hanging above them: "Ticket Office", "Waiting Room" and "Station Master's Office". The windows were broken and there was ivy growing up the walls, but the roofs still looked solid and weatherproof. The space around the buildings was big, about half the size of the school footy pitch, Karl guessed. It was completely overgrown, but where brambles and nettles would grow, so would grass for animals to graze. As the children wandered about, the dreams they'd had since the first day of Infant School finally seemed within their reach.

They pushed through the jungle of plants and at last reached the side of the canal, where they sat down with their legs dangling over the wall.

"It's brilliant!" said Gemma. "I think there could be enough grazing in summer for a couple of sheep."

"The ticket office would make a great cowshed," said Karl.

"We could have ducks on the canal," said Gemma, "once we've got the shopping trolley out, of course."

That was when they heard the growl and turned round to see a huge black dog with a row of very big teeth showing in an extremely fierce snarl.

"Just for show, eh?" said Gemma.

"Nice doggy, nice, nice, *nice* doggy," breathed Meera.

The "doggy" wasn't impressed; he snarled

and growled some more and began to close in.

"We'll have to jump in the canal if he gets any closer," said Gemma.

"We'll be stabbed by a rusty shopping trolley!" squealed Meera.

"Meera, quick!" said Karl. "Give me the jelly babies!"

Two minutes later, the "fierce" guard dog was wagging his tail and begging for another sweet. Karl scratched him behind the ears.

"There's a good boy," said Karl.

The dog whined and offered his paw.

"I think he's lonely," said Gemma.

"He won't be lonely when he's the Silver Street Farm Dog!" said Meera as she patted the dog's huge head.

"The *what* farm dog?" Gemma and Karl said together.

"Oh, I forgot to tell you! I found this nailed to the back of an old bench. It's the station name." Meera reached into her backpack and pulled out an enamel sign that said "Silver Street" in black letters. "It's perfect for our farm."

"Silver Street Farm," said Karl. "Yeah, I like it."

"Silver Street sounds a bit like a shopping centre to me," Gemma grinned. "But it's OK."

They fought their way back through the bramble jungle and climbed out over the gate. The dog stuck his nose through the bars and they fed him one last green jelly baby. He wagged his tail at them as they walked away.

"I think he knows we're coming back!" said Gemma.

Chapter Five

As soon as Karl opened the door to the flat, he knew something was wrong. There was a horrible smell for a start and he could hear his auntie talking crossly in Russian in the sitting room. Then he noticed the newspapers spread all over the floor, decorated with little brown currants and round damp patches. He didn't have to wonder what had been pooing and weeing all over his home for long though, because just as he closed the front door behind him, two fluffy little lambs ran into the hall.

"Baaa!" said the lambs. *"Baaaaaaaaaaa!"*

Auntie Nat was following close behind, bending over the lambs and offering them food from a bowl with "DOG" written on the side.

"Ah, Karl!" Auntie Nat looked at him with a big smile. "At last, I have poodles. Puppies. Bargain from Internet."

"Baaaaaa!" said the "puppies" together, more loudly than ever.

"This one," said Auntie Nat pointing to the larger lamb, "is Bitzi and the other one, little one, is Bobo."

Karl nodded. He didn't know what to say. Auntie Nat waved the dog bowl around.

"I get puppy food," she said, "but they don't like." Auntie Nat's beaming smile faded. "If they don't eat, they die," she said. Suddenly she looked almost as forlorn as the lambs.

"Don't worry, auntie," said Karl, finding his voice at last, "I'll sort them out."

The baby bottles were the easy part. Mr Khan's corner shop had them hanging up behind the counter, next to the aspirins and plasters. Karl bought two. But what to put *in* the bottles was much more tricky.

He spent ages looking at the cartons of milk in the cooler. There was "skimmed", "semi-skimmed", "organic" – but none of them were "sheep's". He peered into the deep-freeze, but saw nothing that seemed to have anything to do with sheep, apart from a packet of frozen lamb chops.

When he got to the checkout, one of Mr Khan's nephews was on the till.

"Excuse me," said Karl. "Do you have any other sorts of milk?"

"What?" said the young man, scowling.

"Milk from – um – other animals."

"What d'you mean, *other animals*?" the boy said, scowling even more. "You taking the mickey?"

Just as Karl was wishing that the floor would swallow him up, Mr Khan himself appeared.

"Ah!" he said kindly, sweeping his grumpy nephew to one side. "Karl! How is your aunt?"

"She's well, thanks, Mr Khan."

"And you were looking for?"

Karl was aware that now everyone in the queue was listening to him.

"Sheep's milk, Mr Khan," Karl said in a very small voice, expecting the shopkeeper to burst into laughter or throw him out for cheek.

"Sheep's milk. Yes," said Mr Khan, as if it

were the most normal thing in the world. "So good for the digestion. Also for complaints of the skin. Your aunt is quite well, I hope?"

For a split second, Karl thought of explaining about the poodle puppies that were really sheep, but it was just much easier to say, "She's fine, Mr Khan. Just a bit of eczema."

"Well, we can't have that. Please come this way."

Mr Khan rummaged around in the freezer and pulled out a bag of frozen white-ish stuff about the size of a football.

"Mr Stephanopolis, may he rest in peace, ordered sheep's milk every week. I hope your aunt finds it beneficial."

Back at the flat, Karl defrosted the milk in the microwave, put some in each of the bottles and together he and Auntie Nat fed the lambs. Karl showed Auntie how to hold the bottle, just as he'd been taught on a school trip to a farm back in year four.

The lambs braced their little legs and sucked hard at the teats, their tiny tails wiggling like demented pipe cleaners. When the bottles had been sucked dry, the lambs became sleepy. Auntie Nat picked up Bobo and Karl took Bitzi onto his lap; the lamb nibbled at his sleeve and closed its eyes with pleasure as he scratched its nubbly little head.

"So cute!" smiled Auntie Nat. Karl nodded and smiled back. They *were* cute. They were *gorgeous*, but in a minute he was going to have to tell Auntie Nat that they *weren't* puppies and he didn't know how he was going to do it.

"Karl," said his auntie, gently stroking

a lamb under the chin, "while you are out, I look on Internet. I check pictures of poodles. These are not poodles. These are sheeps."

Karl sighed.

"Yes, Auntie. I know."

"You think I am foolish?"

"No, Auntie. You've never seen a poodle up close." said Karl. "And anyway," he added, "there's nothing foolish about having a dream."

Chapter Six

While Karl was delving into the freezer with Mr Khan, Gemma was sweeping fur and fluff from the floor of the vet's waiting room.

She worked there two evenings a week, mostly cleaning and tidying, but sometimes she got to help with the animals.

"Gemma!" Mr Sweeney stepped into the waiting room. Gemma liked old Mr Sweeney.

Of all the vets, he let her work with the animals the most. He was holding a small basket with five pale blue eggs inside.

"Mrs Tasker brought them in for me. She knows I like duck eggs," said Mr Sweeney. "But, bless her, she's a bit loopy, and I'm pretty sure they're off. Can you chuck them in the green bin on your way out?"

"Yes," Gemma said, "of course."

"Thanks, Gemma. Next time I have to hold a hamster down, you're the one I'll call!" He grinned through his beard and went back to the consulting room.

Gemma looked at the eggs. They didn't look off. In fact, they looked beautiful, resting in a little nest of snowy feathers. She couldn't bear to chuck them in the bin and hear them smash on the bottom. Very carefully, she

wrapped the eggs in her sweatshirt and went home.

In the middle of the night, a tiny sound woke Gemma up.

"Peep!"

Then, "Peep! Peep!"

The sounds were coming from under her sweatshirt on the floor. The eggs! She'd been so busy all evening being annoyed by her brother, Lee, that she'd forgotten all about them.

She got out of bed and, very gently, she pulled back the sweatshirt and peered at the eggs. A little flake of shell had fallen from the middle of the biggest one, and a beak, a patch of pink skin and some wet yellow fluff showed through the hole. The eggs weren't off – they were just ready to hatch!

"Peep! Peep!" called the duckling from inside.

"Peep!" called another duckling from a different egg. Another flake of shell came off one of the other eggs with a tiny *crack*, and there was such a chorus of peeping that Gemma couldn't tell which eggs were talking and which weren't. Very gently, she lifted one to her ear and listened. Up against her ear she could hear little tapping sounds as the duckling's beak worked at the inside of its shelly prison.

"Hello!" she whispered.

"Peep!" the duckling answered softly. Gemma was so surprised she almost dropped the egg. She tried again, a little louder this time.

"Hello!" she said.

"Peep!" replied the duckling.

Gemma spoke to the other eggs one by

one, until she'd a had a little conversation with all five of them. Then she sat with the basket on her lap and watched as more and more flakes of shell fell off. One of the eggs split right round the middle! The duckling inside slowly pushed the two halves apart and then struggled up on its leathery webbed feet. It shook its beak and looked right at her with its bright, dark eyes.

"Hello, duckling!" said Gemma.

"Peep, peep," said the duckling. It was wet and bedraggled-looking and Gemma realized that it would soon get very cold if it didn't dry out. She got a cardboard box down from her wardrobe, lined it with old newspapers, and put her desk lamp on the floor, so that its warm bulb could shine inside the box and heat up the air.

By the time she got back to the ducklings, the first one had four little damp companions! She put them all inside the box to get warm and they peep-peeped anxiously.

"Hush, ducklings!" Gemma soothed and, as she spoke to them, they settled down. The ducklings all sat on their feet and closed their eyes in the warmth of lamp, like sunbathers. Soon they were drying out and becoming as yellow and fluffy as ducklings on an Easter card.

Gemma knew that newly hatched chicks didn't need to eat or drink for a few hours, so she didn't need to worry about feeding them until the morning. She pulled the box and lamp close to her bed, so she could check on the ducklings and speak to them in the night. Then she fell back into bed.

"Night night, Silver Street Ducks," Gemma whispered sleepily as she closed her eyes.

"Peep, peep, peep, peep," the ducklings whispered back.

Chapter Seven

The next morning, Meera ran all the way to the park where she was meeting Karl, Gemma and the very first Silver Street livestock. Karl was already there, with the lambs on leads looking *very* like puppies.

"I had to carry them some of the way," said Karl, "but they don't seem to mind the collars and leads at all."

Gemma arrived a few moments later, with the ducklings tucked up in her T-shirt.

"They won't let me out of their sight," she giggled. "I had to have them in the shower with me this morning!"

The children sat on the grass while the ducklings tootled about between their legs and the lambs took turns to nibble their hair and butt them playfully. It was hard to stop smiling and concentrate.

"The problem is," Gemma said, "Mum says I can't keep the ducklings. I've got to find them a home by the end of the week…"

"Yeah," said Karl. "Now Auntie Nat knows they're sheep, she doesn't really want them in the flat. You can't house-train lambs. The whole place smells of sheep poo!"

"We need Silver Street right *now*!" Gemma said.

"But it could take months or even years to persuade the council that a city farm is a good idea," said Karl, taking his fringe out of Bobo's mouth.

"Hmmm," said Meera thoughtfully. "What we need is publicity."

"Yes!" said Karl. "If we get everybody in Lonchester on our side then the Council would *have* to give us Silver Street."

"Cosmic TV!" said Gemma. "They're always asking for community stories."

Meera jumped up. "And these are *brilliant* stories ... the great poodle-lamb swindle and the rotten eggs that turned into ducklings!

Come on, if we walk across the park now, we might be in time for their morning news."

Sashi, the young reporter at Cosmic TV, was delighted. It was the best story they'd had in months, she said. Within five minutes, the children and the animals were lined up in the studio. It wasn't much more than a broom cupboard with lights, but it didn't matter. Meera and Karl held a lamb each and the five ducklings popped their heads out of Gemma's T-shirt.

"Looks good!" said Stewy the cameraman, peering through his dreadlocks with a grin. "Looks really, *really* good!"

"If we get this right," said Meera, "the city council should give us Silver Street Farm tied up with a ribbon!"

"OK, everybody!" said Sashi. "On air in

five, four…" she counted the last three seconds with her fingers.

A little red light lit up on Stewy's camera.

Sashi smiled into the camera and began to speak: "Three Lonchester children have big plans to make the derelict station at Silver Street into Lonchester's first city farm," she told the camera. "The city council may have other plans for the old station, but two extraordinary twists of fate have given the children a head start with *their* plans, and provided them with their first farm animals!"

Then Sashi asked Karl about the poodle-lambs and how Auntie Nat had been tricked, while he and Meera fed the lambs with a bottle. She asked Gemma about the "off" eggs that the vet was going to throw out, which had hatched into ducklings, while Gemma held a duckling and stroked its fluffy yellow head.

Then Sashi turned to Meera. "Why do you want to make Silver Street Station into a city farm?" she asked.

For a moment, Meera's head swam with all the dreams and plans that she and Gemma and Karl had made since they were small. Then, suddenly, she knew just what to say.

"Ever since we were in Infants, we've dreamt about making a farm in the city," she began. "We want all Lonchester children to come to Silver Street Farm and see what farm animals are like, so that no one grows up thinking that eggs come from a box and milk comes from a carton."

"Well, you heard it here first!" said Sashi, "More from Cosmic TV News at three."

The red light went off.

"That was brilliant, kids!" said Sashi. "This story is going to be *so* big!"

"Yeah! Big! *So* big," said Stewy. "Can I hold a duckling now?"

Chapter Eight

Sashi was right. The story spread through the city like wildfire.

Within hours, every TV and radio station was talking about it. Rockin' Roland Rogers, Lonchester City FM's most famous DJ, even hosted a phone-in about it.

"So," said Rockin' Roland, "Mrs O from Hopdown Flats, what would *you* like to say about these crazy kids and their plan to make old Silver Street Station into a farm?"

"I think it's wonderful," said Mrs O in a shaky, old lady's voice. "It's not just the kiddies who would enjoy having farm animals at Silver Street. Us oldies would love it, too!"

"Jack Flash now on line three," said Rockin' Roland.

"It's, like, brilliant," said Jack. "Totally cool. I mean, the poodles being sheep, that was bad, but now kinda good. Yeah? Like, wow!"

"And just one more call. Hello, Jody on line two."

"If the council doesn't give Silver Street Station to the kids, I won't vote for them," said Jody, sounding very determined.

"Fighting talk there, Jody. And now for some music. The new single from Fake Tat—"

But the children didn't have time to watch TV or listen to the radio, because soon after the very first broadcast on Cosmic TV, things got busy.

Meera, Gemma and Karl were all at Gemma's house, so the lambs could run about on the tiny bit of lawn and the ducklings could swim in the old paddling pool, when Meera's mobile rang. The only people who ever called her on her mobile were Karl and Gemma, so it was bit of shock.

"Hello, Meera speaking!" said Meera, trying to sound grown-up.

"Hi Meera. It's Sashi from Cosmic TV." She sounded very stressed. "I think you guys need to get back down here. Somebody's just delivered ten bales of hay and—" Sashi took a deep breath—"some chickens and *two real live goats*!"

* * *

The pavement outside Cosmic TV was blocked with a pet carrier full of clucking chickens and a huge pile of hay bales. Standing on top of the bales, contentedly munching hay, were two goats. One was pure white with sticky-up ears and the other was chocolate brown with droopy ears.

"Wow!" said Gemma, who had been reading up about goat breeds. "A Saanen and an Anglo-Nubian!"

But before the children had time to say hello to Silver Street's first goats, Sashi rushed up looking very worried,

"We're in trouble," she said and pointed to a very large, very round police officer who was standing by the hay bales. "I think you'd better speak to him."

Nervously, the three children approached

the officer. Close up, they could see that he was even bigger and even crosser than he had at first appeared, but the moment he saw the children, the lambs and the ducklings, his face broke into a big beaming smile.

"Ah!" he said, as if seeing the children and their animals was the biggest treat of his day. "I wondered when you'd get here!"

The police officer held out a huge hand for the children to shake. "I'm Sergeant Short," he said. "And I presume you're the youngsters who want to turn Silver Street Station into a city farm?"

Caught in Sergeant Short's blue-eyed stare, the children could only nod.

"Well," he said quietly, leaning down from his great height so they could hear him whisper, "strictly off the record, I think that's a great idea, but—" he added straightening up to his official height again— "we can't have goats and bales obstructing the public highway. So my fellow officers and I will help you to get it all moved." And the sergeant gave the children the biggest wink they'd ever seen.

Sergeant Short asked Sashi not to film the hay bales, chickens, lambs, goats and ducklings being loaded into the back of a big police van by four police officers.

"Not sure how the chief super would see it, really," he said. "Best keep it between us, eh?"

"Hop in!" said a young woman police officer with a big smile. She helped the children into the van and they were off.

The children were too astonished to ask where they were being taken. Karl wondered anxiously if it was all just a trick and if they were about to go to prison. But when the doors opened, they found themselves at the far end of the park. The police had built a little compound for the animals, using crash barriers and crowd-control netting.

In just a few minutes, the goats were happily nibbling hay and the chickens were scratching in the shade of the trees.

"You can't stay here long," said the Sergeant, "but I've cleared it with the chief super until tomorrow. In the meantime, Julie – I mean PC Worthing – will help keep an eye on things."

Julie leaned out of the driver's seat of the van.

"Sarge? Sarge! You need to see this!"

On a tiny television in the front of the

police van, the Wire TV lunchtime news was just ending.

"We now bring you a live announcement from Lonchester City Council," the newscaster was saying. The picture cut to a big man in a suit, standing outside the City Hall.

He looked *very* cross indeed.

"I would like to read the following statement from Lonchester City Council," the man began, already rather red in the face. "The Council has for some time been planning to demolish Silver Street Station, in preparation for a new multi-story car park."

Meera gasped. Auntie Priya hadn't told her *that!*

"Lonchester City Council would like to reassure tax payers that there are no plans *whatsoever* to make this site into a city farm."

As he said the words "city farm," he made a face as if, Gemma thought, he'd swallowed a wasp.

"Furthermore," he said, now looking so red that Karl wondered if he might explode, "we have decided to begin the demolition of Silver Street Station tomorrow at nine a.m. Thank you."

PC Worthing turned off the television. She seemed almost as upset as the children.

"Oh, dear," she said. "Oh dear, oh dear."

Gemma buried her nose in a duckling's comforting fluff and Karl and Meera held the lambs extra close. Nobody said anything.

"All right," said Sergeant Short. "I'll admit that it doesn't look good…"

The children shook their heads in gloomy agreement.

"But, you know what they say," he winked one of his huge winks, "it's not over till the fat policeman sings."

Chapter Nine

Sergeant Short and his officers set up crash barriers as pens for the animals (PC Worthing was particularly good with the goats). They carried bales and fetched buckets of water from the fountain so the animals wouldn't go thirsty. They even made the children a sort of tent from silvery emergency blankets, so they could spend the night with their makeshift farm in the park.

Just as the first story about Silver Street Station had spread, so did the news about the mini farm camped out in the park and the city council's promise to demolish Silver Street Station. By early evening, the children were surrounded by a curious crowd and a flock of TV and radio reporters waving cameras and microphones.

In spite of what the council had said about making Silver Street Station into a car park, people still wanted to hear about the children's plans for a city farm. But answering the questions from the interviewers and the crowd made it all seem even more sad. Tomorrow, Silver Street Station would be flattened, no matter what the children's plans had been, and all their new-found animals would be homeless.

"OK, ladies and gents," Sergeant Short said at last, "just one more question, then I think these young people should get some rest and you all need to go home!"

The reporter from City Wire TV pushed through the crowds and shoved a big fluffy microphone under Meera's nose.

"I'd like to ask," he said, with a nasty sneer, "what's going to happen to all your fine plans when Silver Street Station is demolished tomorrow? Aren't you just some rather foolish children with an even more foolish dream?"

The crowd gasped and there were even a few quiet "boo"s.

Meera looked up at the reporter. Maybe he was right, she thought. Maybe all this time, ever since Gemma, Karl and she had been friends, it had all been a silly, hopeless dream.

For the first time in her life, Meera was lost for words; her mouth opened like a goldfish's, but nothing would come out.

"Well," said the reporter smugly, "I think *that's* your answer!"

"Oh no, it isn't," said Gemma, stepping up to him, ducklings peep-peeping from inside her shirt. "We may be kids, but we aren't foolish. A city farm is a really, *really* good idea."

The crowd murmured its approval.

"And do you know what?" said Karl. His voice wobbled a little, but it was still loud. "Maybe Silver Street Station *won't* be demolished."

"Well said!" cried several people in the crowd.

Meera looked at Karl and Gemma and was suddenly ashamed of giving in so easily. She jumped onto a hay bale so that she was eye to eye with the reporter, and she spoke out so that everyone could hear her.

"Yes," she said. "That's right! Maybe tomorrow morning the people of Lonchester will decide that they don't want *another* car park and that they'd *much* rather have a city farm instead!"

The whole crowd exploded with cheering, as if they'd just been holding it in all along. The reporter scowled and slunk away.

Still standing on her hay bale, Meera could see that her parents, Auntie Nat and Gemma's brother Lee were waiting for them at the back of the crowd. And they were cheering loudest of all.

Chapter Ten

Almost as soon as the pink dawn light touched the tops of the trees at the edge of the park, people began to arrive. Sergeant Short wasn't in the least surprised. He knew his city and he knew when something big was going to happen.

At 6.30 a.m. he asked Julie to heat some water for tea, then he woke the children, who had spent the night curled up in a nest of hay bales under their silver "tent" with the ducklings and the poodle-lambs.

Meera opened her eyes. She saw the tree tops, the blue sky and Sergeant Short's big, beaming face looking down at her.

"Time to meet your supporters," he said. "Told you it wasn't over till the fat policeman sings."

Meera sat up and rubbed her eyes, then she rubbed them again. This *had* to be a dream. She nudged Gemma and kicked Karl in the leg, rather harder than she'd meant to out of sheer astonishment.

Beyond the crash barriers, hundreds and hundreds of people of all ages, shapes and sizes stood quietly waiting. Many carried home-made banners saying "SILVER STREET FARM" and "WE WANT A FARM NOT A CAR PARK", or simply showing pictures of farm animals.

"We've done it!" breathed Karl. "We've got the whole city behind us!"

"If we arrive at Silver Street Station with all this lot," said Gemma, "*nothing's* going to be demolished!"

Meera climbed onto the hay bales and called out, "Good morning, everybody!" to the crowd.

"Good morning!" they called back. And, as if Meera's "good morning" had flipped a switch, the whole park suddenly seemed to wake up. Everyone began to talk at once. People worked on their banners, drank from flasks, ate sandwiches and jumped up and down to warm up in the chilly early morning air.

More and more people began to arrive: Auntie Nat, with a flask of hot chocolate and home-made rolls to dip in it ("So exciting," she said. "My Karl and his friends all celebrities now, eh?"); Meera's mum and dad and her three little brothers, with a banner attached to the buggy saying "Silver Street City Farm" in letters made of baking foil; Lee and his mates, dressed up as animals (three chickens, one sheep and something that might have been a zebra or a tiger or possibly just a stripy caterpillar).

Finally, Gemma's dad turned up with his accordian and started singing "Silver Street's a City Farm" to the tune of "Old MacDonald Had a Farm". Lots of people joined in, so Gemma couldn't be embarrassed.

Then Sergeant Short spoke to the crowd through the megaphone.

"Citizens of Lonchester," he began, so sternly that everyone immediately became very quiet, "it is the duty of the Lonchester Police Force to uphold the law. So I must ask you now to leave the park."

There were a few cries of "Shame!" but the Sergeant held up his hand for silence. "However, if you wish to make your way to Silver Street Station, I will be obliged to provide a full police escort, to make sure that nobody gets into any trouble."

Only Meera was close enough to see the twinkle in Sergeant Short's eye as he spoke, but the crowd understood anyway.

And that was how Meera, Karl and Gemma led a procession of ducklings, sheep-poodles, goats, chickens and cheering Lonchester citizens across the city to Silver Street Station, with twenty police officers as a guard of honour.

Chapter Eleven

The protesters sang at the top of their voices, all the way from the park.

"Silver Street's a city farm

Ee-i, ee-i, oh!

And on that farm we'll have some sheep

Ee-i, ee-i, oh!"

Gemma's dad's accordian was joined by

Mr Khan's trombone, a pair of cymbals and some sleighbells that were being shaken very enthusiastically by the oldest of Meera's little brothers. Even some of the police officers were humming along.

All the people standing outside the gates of Silver Street must have heard them coming for *ages* because the man from the council, the digger drivers, and a whole lot of other people wearing hard hats and fluorescent waistcoats were just standing and staring, frozen to the spot, as the procession came down the street.

The protesters finished the last verse in four part harmony:

"Silver Street's a city farm

Ee-i, eeeeeee-iiiiiii, oooooooohhhh!"

Mr Khan added a lovely little trombone solo right at the end, as they all stopped just millimetres from the workers and the man from the council in his grey suit.

For a moment, nobody said anything, apart from the lambs who said, "baaaaa", as it was time for another bottle feed, and the goats who said, "meeeeeh!", because they were fed up of Meera pulling on their leads, and the ducklings who "peep-peeped" to be let out of Gemma's T-shirt.

Then, the man from the council – who was, Karl noticed, already going red again – cleared his throat. "If you think all this *nonsense*," he said, waving his hand at all the people and their banners, "is going to have the *slightest* effect on the council's decision, then think again!" He shoved an official-looking document under Meera's nose. "This demolition notice gives me the right to flatten this ruin *right now*!" he said, adding under his breath with what could only be described as a snarl, "and there's nothing you kids and your *stupid, mindless, ridiculous* protest can do about it!"

"Ah, Councillor Newberry!" said Sashi, popping up out of the crowd with Stewy and his camera at her side. She pushed a microphone under the councillor's nose. "We've got your comments on tape," she said, smiling innocently. "So I was just wondering if you were officially describing all these good people as 'ridiculous' and 'stupid' and – what was it – 'mindless'?"

"Were you?" demanded the crowd.

"I represent many small businesses in the city," said Mr Khan, "and I'm sure we wouldn't want to be called *stupid*."

"Noooo!" booed the crowd.

"A city farm is a great community project," said Meera's mother. "It's very far from mindless or ridiculous."

"That's right!" cheered the crowd.

"In fact," Meera said, "it might be a good idea for you to tear up that demolition notice right now…"

"Yes," Gemma added. "And let all these people help us build our very first city farm!"

Councillor Newberry turned as pale as he'd been red. He dropped the piece of paper and opened the locked gates without another word.

Silver Street Station's new future rushed in and one very happy ex-guard dog ran out, delighted to see his three friends once again.

Chapter Twelve

By the end of the day, the old station was transformed. Roofs were patched, windows had new glass and there was even running water and electricity in the old station master's office. The lambs had a stall to sleep in and a fenced yard where they could gambol about. The old signal box had been made into a chicken house, with perches and a nest box to lay eggs in. The goats had been given a rather overgrown enclosure between the old railway lines and were already doing a good job of eating some of the bigger bushes. Several supermarket trolleys had been pulled from the canal, but the ducklings hadn't taken a swim. They were too busy being chased about by their new foster mum, a hen called Mavis, who was so motherly that she didn't notice her new children were ducks, not chickens.

It had been an incredible day. But there was one more incredible thing in store. She stepped out of a rickety little camper van, with a sheepdog following right behind her and marched straight up to the children, who were stacking bales outside the lambs' stall in the old waiting room.

"I'm Flora," the girl said in a broad Scots accent, "and I'm going to manage your farm."

Her mouth was set in straight line and her bright blue eyes blazed with determination.

"Um..." said Meera. "I thought *we'd* manage the farm."

"You can't," Flora said simply, pushing her mad curly black hair out of her eyes. "There's got to be somebody here 24/7. And you'll be back in school in a week or two. What then? No, no, you definitely need me."

"But where will you live?" Karl asked.

"In my van, of course!" said Flora, as if Karl was two.

"We can't pay you..." said Gemma.

"Och, don't worry about that. I've money of my own, I don't need anyone else's."

The children looked at each other and smiled.

"Good," said Flora, smiling back. "That's

settled then! Oh, there's just one more thing," she added. "It's my dog here, Flinty. She's rubbish with sheep, but she's a first-class chicken herder. Is that OK with you?"

"Fine!" said Karl laughing.

"Perfect!" said Gemma.

"Flora," said Meera, "I think a sheepdog that herds chickens is going to fit right in.

Welcome to Silver Street Farm!"